M000100908

A Movie Lover's Search for Romance

Joanna J. Charnas

Copyright 2020 by MSI Press LLC

All rights reserved. No part of this book may be reproduced or utilized in any form
or by any means, electronic or mechanical, including photocopying, recording,
or by any information storage and retrieval system, without permission in writing
from the publisher.

For information, contact

MSI Press, LLC
1760 Airline Hwy, #203
Hollister, CA 95023

Library of Congress Control Number: 2020930771

ISBN: 978-1-950328-06-2

DEDICATION

For Jonathan Charnas, in deep gratitude for his special brand of avuncular love.

Table of Contents

ACKNOWLEDGMENTS

I want to thank the following people for their support of this book: my late father, Stephen Charnas, who encouraged me to publish when I was writing for my own amusement; my stepmother, Suzy McKee Charnas, who generously offered her professional advice; my uncle, Jonathan Charnas; my brother and sister-in-law, Charles N. Charnas and Margaret Charnas; my godmother, Meryl Cohen; my surrogate aunt, Sheila Hochman; Candace Bremond; Pieter Estersohn; Kris Franey; Daniel Hays; Mrs. Careth Ried; and Roberta Strebel.

I want to extend special thanks to my editor, Cathy A. Kodra, and my publicist, Laurie Graff.

And to all the men who made me feel valued and loved—thank you.

INTRODUCTION

This book recalls my search for love in my forties and fifties. For several years after my divorce at forty-one, my love life was slim to none. I focused on my career, buying my first home, and settling into it. I dated sporadically, but none of the men I went out with were particularly memorable. I didn't care. My love life wasn't my priority. I went to work and to the movies, and I was fine. Then, I saw *The Pianist* in late 2002, and the performance of Adrian Brody as the main character awakened something in me. My crazy post-divorce, romantic life began with that film.

Movies and men became the focus of my wild middle-age dating life. Initially, I fell sway to three ridiculous crushes: first, Adrien Brody; next, my father's friend, twenty-five years my senior; and finally, my Adonis-like washing machine repairman. As I pondered these crushes, they reminded me of scenes and characters from the thousands of movies I'd watched obsessively since starting high school. The movies provided a frame of reference for the jumble of emotions and events I experienced.

Then, after a three-year, post-divorce dry spell, my love life suddenly and inexplicably took off. I dated a spectacular array of romantic prospects, including an Orthodox Jew, a recent Iranian immigrant, a severely disabled man, and a man sixteen years younger than me who badly wanted in my pants. I opened myself to any reasonable option, trying to understand what I wanted from a partner. I looked to the movies for guidance and succor with each new adventure. Cinema was my touchstone, and, unlike men, movies rarely let me down.

As months passed, I reflected on larger issues: whether to remain friends with romantic rejects, how I felt about television advertisements for erectile dysfunction medications shown during the dinner hour, and the world of all matters kinky. I considered my previous experiences with these issues and reviewed cinematic references, such as 1978's *Coming Home*, a film that depicts the complications of relationships, sex, and paraplegia. Afterward, I resolved not to befriend my ex-boyfriends, to be open to sexual adventure, and to live in hope that the networks would stop running ads for ED medications at six o'clock.

After dating enough eager men to populate a baseball lineup, I consider the effects of my newly slimmed body and recently discovered hotness, as well as the downfall of being smart and verbal in the dating world.

As I drew closer to finding a mate, the vicissitudes of dating became increasingly wearing. I once found myself crying for days when a second date didn't transpire. At times, I thought I'd lost my mind. While still referring to movies and taking comfort and guidance from them, their ability to soothe me waned.

Then I met Simon. He was everything I wanted and more, until he wasn't. After five years, our relationship ended. Once again—now at age fifty—I renewed my search for love with confidence and movies to guide me.

After I broke up with Simon, I needed a hiatus from dating. But a year after we parted, my romantic life exploded again. I felt I was in some throwback to adolescence although, as one friend observed, adolescent dating never looked like my adult love life. I thought back to my dating experiences after my divorce and culled whatever wisdom I could from them. I repeated some old mistakes, made new ones, and continued to learn what I wanted from romance, always looking to the movies for references and solace, my lifelong habit.

I hope this book's readers will relate to my experiences and find comfort knowing they are not alone in their quest for love. I also hope they understand that art, in film or in myriad other forms, can provide a touchstone and comfort. My wish is that readers will laugh along with me as they share in my adventures, successes, and lessons learned.

Chapter 1, 2003

ADRIEN: LOSING MY MIND

Early this spring my friend Candace called to tell me she had recorded the previous night's episode of Saturday Night Live for me. She explained that the object of my "crush" and winner of this year's Academy Award for Best Actor, Adrien Brody, had hosted the show. Not wanting to be unkind, I thanked her for the thoughtfulness but felt compelled to correct her.

"I think we need to call this by its proper name: my pathetic, middle-aged, divorcée's crush."

Candace, knowing the truth when she heard it, didn't argue the point.

How did I, at the age of forty-three, find myself with a serious crush on this particular young actor? I ask myself this often. I've been in love with movies for thirty years. I easily passed for eighteen by the time I started high school, and I could gain entry into any film I wanted to see without an adult escort. During my adolescence, I planned all my free time around movies. I saw my five-hundredth movie when I turned twenty-one and then stopped counting. (In the 1970s, video, DVDs, and live streaming didn't exist. Only theaters showed new releases.) Movies have been one of the primary constants in my life. When I'm happy, when I'm sad, when times are great, and when they're awful, I go to the movies. They help me relax, feel a range of emotions, and think about people and life outside my own existence. When I can't make it to a movie for more than a few weeks, I become cranky, as if I abruptly stopped taking a necessary medication.

3

But for the last thirty years, I haven't had a single crush on an actor. I've followed actors' careers, and I've appreciated their physical attributes. Like many other straight women in America, I inhaled deeply the first time I saw Brad Pitt in *Thelma and Louise*. But until now, I hadn't felt the true tingling of a completely irrational attraction.

In 1999, my former husband and I took in a bargain matinee of *Summer of Sam*. The movie had received mixed reviews, but I'm a huge fan of the director, Spike Lee, and my motto is "never trust a critic." Neither my husband nor I was prepared for the power of the film. An elderly man who'd seen it by himself engaged us in conversation as we left the movie. He continued to gush about it for five minutes outside the theater. He told us he loved it so much, he just needed to talk about it with someone. We loved it, too, and didn't mind chatting with him.

Before *Summer of Sam*, I'd never noticed Adrien Brody although I'd seen him in small roles in other films. I found him compelling in his role as Richie, the aspiring punk rocker, and I remember hoping to see more of him soon in other films.

For three-and-a-half years, I waited. My Uncle Jon went to an early New York screening of *The Pianist* and insisted I see it. I was thrilled Adrien Brody had the lead role of Wladyslaw Szpilman, the Polish Holocaust survivor. I saw the movie as soon as it was released in San Diego, my hometown, and found Adrien's performance deeply stirring. My pathetic crush began.

What happened to me? Although he's attractive, Adrien doesn't have standard movie star good looks. Surely it made more sense to swoon over actors like George Clooney or Antonio Banderas, more classic Hollywood glamour boys who are closer to my age. Perhaps Adrien's beautiful black hair, which he wore slicked back at the beginning and the end of *The Pianist*, ignited my crush. My father has dark coloring and black hair. Am I at the mercy of something embarrassingly Oedipal? It's a reasonable theory.

In my twenties and thirties, I dated a couple of guys with Adrien's tall, rangy build and broad shoulders tapering to a trim waist. Maybe I'm unconsciously longing for the romances of youth. Or am I captivated by the profound soulfulness of Adrien's performance? At the beginning of *The Pianist*, he looked as natty as Humphrey Bogart in his prime. As the movie progressed, Adrien looked increasingly like a rabid rat. Throughout, he conveyed his character's fundamental humanity, all of it accomplished with little dialogue. I like this theory better. It would be more flattering to think that I'm in the grips of a transcendent performance.

Despite the Vegas odds-makers, I wasn't surprised when Adrien won the Academy Award for Best Actor in a leading role. I've watched the Oscar telecast every year since 1971, and I like to flatter myself that I understand the voting patterns of Academy members. I screamed when he won. The beautiful acceptance speech Adrien delivered when he received his award did nothing to subdue my crush. The United States had been fighting the war in Afghanistan for two-and-a-half years by the night of the awards, March 24, 2003. The war in Iraq began just a few days earlier. Who among us didn't feel our hearts tug when Adrien made a plea for peace and mentioned his buddy, Tommy, in Kuwait? Whatever remained of my equilibrium disappeared in those few minutes.

After the Oscars, I had myself a little Adrien Brody film festival. I watched all two hours and forty-five minutes of *The Thin Red Line,* an epic World War II movie. I searched for Adrien, who, as it turned out, was mostly left on the proverbial cutting-room floor. He had about three minutes of face time in that movie, which is probably why I didn't remember him. Then I rented *Liberty Heights,* a lovely little Barry Levinson movie I'd somehow missed when it was released. In this film, Adrien plays the older son of a Jewish family in 1950s Baltimore. He lusts after a beautiful blond girl from the other side of town and appears on screen in his undershirt. I enjoyed *Liberty Heights* immensely.

Next, I rented *Summer of Sam,* which I hadn't viewed since 1999. It was just as good as I recalled. Adrien is sometimes shirtless in this film. Last, I rented *The Affair of the Necklace,* a movie I probably would have skipped had it not been for Adrien's presence. In this movie, Adrien's clothes remain on, but he plays a European count with a nifty accent and long black hair hanging down his back, like a young George Washington.

I enjoyed my crush and my all-Adrien film festival until the morning I woke up and realized, aghast, that I'd been dreaming about Adrien all night! I had serious concerns that something silly and fun had begun to haunt my dreams. I wondered if this was how stalkers were made. Did crazy ladies with too much cellulite suddenly go over the edge? How could I, a mature person—a social worker, for goodness' sake—have reached this state? Although happy to admire and pine a little, I didn't want to end up as the lead story on *Entertainment Tonight.* Why did a ridiculous crush hold me in its sway *now,* when my life was finally stable and calm?

I'm beginning to think that's exactly the point. At forty-three, I have no real regrets about my love life. I've been deliriously in love more than once, as well as alone and lonely, and everything in between. Two years into my separation and divorce, liberated from the pervasive emotional needs of my youth, I've become a free-range romantic. But I'm fine on my own. I can do and feel whatever I want, including going weak in the knees over a movie star thirteen years my junior.

So, I guess I won't worry about my all-night Adrien Brody phantasmagoria. Adrien's mother has declared she thinks he's beautiful, and so do I. He is a gifted actor. I'll continue to bask in his celluloid glow whenever the opportunity arises, and he's welcome to invade my dreams. I know that's the closest I'll ever get to him. And when his next movie comes out, whether it's a masterpiece or a mess, I'll be in line to buy a ticket.

HENRY, OR PATHETIC CRUSH #2

Just as my crush on Adrien Brody began to wane, I began crushing on Henry. Henry, as in Henry Cooper, direct descendent of James Fennimore Cooper, who wrote the well-known classic, *The Last of the Mohicans*. Henry Cooper, of the Coopers of Cooperstown. Until I met Henry, I'd never actually heard anyone who sounded like George Plimpton. I thought that high, guttural, WASP accent was an anachronism, like hula-hoops and the Ed Sullivan Show. If Henry was not the highest of high WASP, he would be a parody of rich Americans. But Henry is the real deal. He has piles of the *Social Register* stacked casually around his living room, along with old copies of *The New Yorker*, for which he once wrote.

Henry is my father's friend. They went to Andover together in the late '40s and early '50s. My father is not high WASP. Dad is the product of four Eastern European Jewish grandparents, each of whom traveled to the United States alone in childhood or early adulthood to make better lives for themselves. Dad will turn seventy in a few months. He's aging beautifully and has less gray hair than I do. Henry is not aging beautifully. He looks like an old professor badly in need of a haircut; his bangs, while still brown, often fall in his eyes. At forty-four, I've been divorced for three years. I've had no major romance in my life since my divorce. Instead, I've been reduced to pining for the old high-school classmate of my father. I'm sure I could go lower on the humiliating divorce scale, but I don't want to think about where or what that might be.

I met Henry when my father and I were in New York to participate in a big family Seder, the Passover meal. When either of us visits New

York, we usually stay with my Uncle Jon, Dad's brother. Jon can only accommodate one of us at a time, and Dad graciously ceded Jon's blow-up air mattress to me. Dad has many old friends in New York with whom he can camp out although he's also happy to stay at a Bed and Breakfast as he had the year before. But Henry had made overtures to Dad to visit him, so Dad stayed at his apartment on 5th Avenue, near the Metropolitan Museum of Art—Jackie O. territory before she died.

On my first day in the city, I agreed to meet Dad at Henry's apartment. I'd never met Henry before. I stepped into a different world upon entering his building, different even from the one I'd just left outside on 5th Avenue. Inside the exquisitely sedate and elegant lobby, there might as well have been a continuous loop over a loudspeaker stating, "Hello, welcome to the world of OLD MONEY." Tasteful wood furniture and beautifully framed prints of well-bred animals, pastoral scenes, and still lifes filled the space. I thought I had stepped into a Woody Allen movie. I could clearly envision Mariel Hemingway in *Manhattan* informing Woody that she couldn't get back together with him because she was about to leave to attend school in London. After I snapped out of my movie reverie, I noticed the building had an inner courtyard lush with blooming plants. The area was breathtakingly serene and lovely. Sight unseen, I might have married Henry right there. We could have held the ceremony in the courtyard and invited the other co-op members so as not to create neighborly animosity.

I once read that Jackie O. didn't keep her belongings in pristine condition, and in fact, they tended to be a little frayed around the edges. The relaxed attitude about maintaining possessions must be attributable to possessing old money. With new money, everything must sparkle. I suppose with old money, one can relax about the details. I contemplated this after leaving the elevator and entering the hallway of Henry's floor. The appointments were lovely, but the paint could have used a touch up.

Dad greeted me at the door and introduced me to Henry. Transfixed by his accent, I had no idea what he said. No doubt something polite and appropriate. He could have been reciting lines from a Harry Potter movie for all I knew.

After introductions, Dad and I set off to enjoy the city. We made plans to meet Henry and Uncle Jon later for lunch at the Trustee's dining room in the Metropolitan, where Henry is a member. At lunch, Henry flirted with me. I made a disparaging remark about my pants, and Henry responded, "Oh, I think you would look good in whatever you wore." Dad and Jon were so preoccupied with the great food, the sublime dining room, and their conversation that Henry's flirting passed them by. I'm a big sucker for a brainy guy, even one who's my father's age. A modicum of flirting and a big dose of smarts will do it for me every time, so Henry was on very solid ground by the end of lunch.

I saw Henry twice more during my trip, each time when I picked up Dad to begin our day together. On one of those mornings, Henry asked me about an invitation he'd received to a social function. The dress code for the function read "festive attire." Henry's divorce had occurred about the same time as mine. His ex-wife must have helped him select party clothes. We both mused about what might constitute "festive attire." Henry thought tweed could be festive. I had my doubts. When I expressed them to Henry, he said, "Oh, tweed can be very festive." All I could think was, in what universe is tweed festive? But I kept my mouth shut. Perhaps if you are a Cooper of Cooperstown, tweed *is* festive. Who would not be smitten with a man who thinks of tweed as party clothes?

On the last day we spent together in the city, Dad disclosed that Henry really liked me. I replied that I really liked Henry, too. But I wasn't ready to admit I had a thing for his old high school friend.

Dad left New York a few days before I did, and I spent the rest of my trip hanging out with Uncle Jon, visiting relatives from the other side of my family, and seeing old friends. But I had Henry on my mind. I wondered what he wore to his party. I wondered if he would flirt with me if we saw each other again. He'd said he wanted to visit the new Disney Symphony Hall in Los Angeles, something I also wanted to do. I fantasized about us going to LA together.

When I returned home to California, I confided in a close friend about my thing for Henry. She said Henry and I should date. This friend has given me bad dating advice for two decades. I refrained from telling her I thought she was stupid. Instead, I patiently explained the geographic distance between Henry and me, along with our age disparity and other impracticalities of her suggestion. I thought about movie romances I might have seen about middle-aged women and elderly men. I couldn't think of one film that depicted a love story with those demographics.

Shortly after my trip, I joined eharmony.com. I've decided to let my membership expire at the end of the month. I've become sick of insensitive, middle-aged men who complain about their exes. Maybe someone

Henry's age would know better than to whine about his former wife. Dating in one's forties, I've learned, is radically different from dating in one's twenties and thirties. When I was younger, I was tolerant of my romantic interests' complaints about their exes. Now I'm old and hardhearted, and I don't want to hear about it, let alone be supportive. I don't care if a guy lost the house, his dog, and half of his 401K. I really don't. I had to pay my ex-husband a lump sum when we divorced. My family was outraged. I just wanted to move on. I wasn't upset about it then, and I'm not upset now. All I want on a date is to enjoy the sushi and flirt a little.

I recently saw a movie that triggered a wellspring of mourning. I'm grieving all of the romances of my youth. I feel self-absorbed and monumentally silly. Usually when you think about people mourning their youth, it conjures up sentiments about lost opportunities. I don't think I missed anything. In fact, looking back, I can't believe how many great romantic experiences I had. I honestly don't know how I was so lucky. But the time since my divorce could most generously be called a dry spell. In the last three years, there have been no brief encounters with men at weddings; no running into someone I once dated casually and enjoying a night of long-delayed consummation; no seasons of sincere, handwritten correspondence from men who live far away; no spiritual encounters in unlikely places with captivating strangers. I am not so much upset about being single now as feeling sad that the phase of easy, optimistic romance has left my life and may never return.

In order to counteract my mourning, I made a list of all men in my life unrelated to me but who love me. Some of these men frequently tell me they love me. The length of the list surprised me. Five of the eight men are straight; three are gay. All but one of the straight men are married or in relationships, but I'm not a threat to their wives or girlfriends. The men include my childhood sweetheart, another old childhood friend, someone who confessed sixteen years ago, while in a car I was driving, that he had "feelings" for me, three former colleagues, and two other ex-loves and friends. I'm in regular contact with most of these men but speak to a couple of them only occasionally. However, I could tell all of them almost anything about my life. Each is a wonderful and close friend.

I decided in order to ease my sadness, I would reach out and feel the love. With several of them, I didn't need to reach out. My childhood sweetheart e-mailed me, which he does regularly. I had dinner with one of my former colleagues, our routine every four to six weeks. I finally caught up with the friend in Florida with whom I was playing phone tag, and the father of my youngest godchild called to thank me for the birthday present I'd sent his son. In the last two weeks, either in the normal course of my life, or because I made a call, I've had contact with six of the eight men. When I told my tale of mourning to a co-worker, she couldn't believe I had eight close male friends. Neither could one of the eight men with whom I discussed my current state of mind. (I even confessed to making the list and told him he was on it, although his appearance was self-evident.) He told me most people are lucky if they have *one* person they can relate to intimately. I had to agree, but the idea comforted me only briefly. As he hung up, he told me he loved me.

I'm still mourning, and I'm still pining for Henry. I've been listening to Bob Dylan's great record from 1975, *Blood on the Tracks*, over and over again. This is an album of the most baleful, beautiful, and sometimes angry love songs imaginable. I'm fairly certain Henry has never willingly listened to *Blood on the Tracks*. Sometimes, a girl just needs a good dose of Dylan.

My father and stepmother visited me recently. I confessed my crush to them and then pined out loud for Henry. I said I could make the last ten years of Henry's life very happy. Dad laughed at my numerous Henry references although he also began to take me seriously. He made an offer to set us up. He even volunteered to make a special trip to New York to make it happen. But I told him I couldn't pursue Henry because his three grown daughters, who no doubt hover near my age, would all hate me. They would think I was only after Henry's money. Dad saw my point.

But I keep thinking about Henry. I recently saw the new movie *Before Sunset*, in which two former lovers meet in Paris and talk nonstop about their past affair and present lives. I asked Dad, via e-mail, if he thought Henry would like to meet me in Paris for a romantic rendezvous. Dad was very encouraging. He wrote back that Henry and I could meet, talk endlessly like the old lovers in the movie, drink coffee at sidewalk cafés, and nap together. It all sounded good to me.

Dad also wrote that Henry would snore, and that I would make fun of his accent. I wrote back that Henry would not snore, and I would never make fun of his accent. Henry's accent is central to my wonderment of him. I told Dad if Henry and I fall in love and marry, I would give each of his daughters notarized copies of our pre-nuptial agreement so they could avoid all worry about their inheritances. After making Henry happy for a decade or two, all I would want upon his demise is the apartment in the divine building and a modest trust fund to pay for the co-op fees. While we were both still healthy, Henry and I would enjoy all the cultural events of the city. I'd go to the opera with him. We'd see many of the independent movies I now attend with my movie buddy or alone. Henry would place his hand in the small of my back when I stepped off the curb. He'd ask my opinion on what to wear to parties. I'd thoughtfully tell him, "No, sweetheart, I don't think tweed is festive enough." We would read *The New Yorker* together and discuss the articles. We'd sleep like spoons. His three middle-aged daughters would see us together and grudgingly acknowledge that I married for love.

Maybe I should let Dad set me up with Henry. Maybe I should get out of the house more often or join a new Internet dating service. Maybe I should give Bob Dylan a rest. Maybe I should call friends number seven and eight on the "men who love me" list to see if talking to them snaps me out of this ridiculous phase. I just don't know.

But in my imagination, I see myself with Henry in Paris. It's Fall. The weather is cool but pleasant. We're drinking heavily sugared coffee with cream. We're chatting about the art we just viewed in some out-of-the-way gallery. Henry absentmindedly touches the back of my hand as he makes a point, and life is good again.

Chapter 3, 2004b

CRUSH #3: THE BLOND GOD

One night last December, I was reminded with searing clarity why people should never run appliances when away from home. I'd been washing my sheets when I heard several strange clicking sounds and then a loud knock. I ran to my washer. When I lifted the lid, thick gray smoke gusted out. I had the presence of mind to turn off the washer, call one of my neighbors to come over to make sure the thing wasn't on fire, and open all the windows. It took several hours for the smoke to clear. My neighbor assured me one of the belts had probably gotten stuck and burned but that the machine was not actually in flames. When the smoke dissipated and I calmed down, I called my appliance repair service. I was deeply relieved when I received an appointment for the next morning.

A year before, when one of my appliances broke, the repair service sent a middle-aged, gray-haired, pudgy man to work on my dryer. He'd been on the brink of divorce with his allegedly alcoholic wife. I had the privilege of hearing the entire sad story of her drunken and fiscal irresponsibility as he fixed my dryer. The repair took two visits, and, on the last one, I sent him off with my overflow of homemade holiday macaroons as well as good wishes for the impending legal battle.

The morning after my washer's belt combusted, I waited for the repairman. When he didn't arrive as expected, I called the company office to make sure I'd understood the appointment time correctly. The office assured me the repairman was on his way. A few minutes later the phone rang, and a man with a thick accent assured me he would be at my condo shortly. I envisioned another middle-aged, overweight man, someone a little raggedy, like an Eastern European immigrant circa turn of the century.

Instead, I opened my front door to a blond god. He told me his name was Radek. I am not partial to blonds. In order for me to be attracted to blond men, they must look like movie stars. Radek *did* look like a movie star, but what first came to mind when I laid eyes on him was, "If Jesus had been blond, he might have looked like *this.*"

Radek appeared to be in his early thirties. He had a broad face with rough but handsome features, wide shoulders, a tapered waist, and not a hint of fat anywhere. The killer feature, the one that entranced me, was the thick, dark-blond hair falling in curls to his shoulders. He had the kind of hair both genders dream of. This was spend-hundreds-of-dollars-a-month-on-it hair, except that his was natural. My impulse was to reach out and touch it, but my semi-sane self prevented me from stroking my repairman's head immediately upon greeting him.

As a social worker, I can converse with almost anyone, even people not completely grounded in reality. I'm good at getting folks to relax and talk. My clients often reveal deeply personal things to me during my first interview with them. I think all good social workers have this skill, and I like to exercise it with my repairmen. I want to know who's in my home.

People will usually open up to you quickly if your interest in them is sincere. While Radek knelt on my floor and took apart my washing machine, I encouraged him to tell me about himself. He said he'd been in the United States for five years. He told me that his father came from Poland to America several years before him and had urged Radek to immigrate too. He seemed wistful about his decision to leave Poland. He said, with a degree of longing that surprised me, "I vas heppy in Polant." I sensed that if he had to do it over again, he wouldn't have left his homeland. Now, he was stuck in a foreign country and wasn't entirely happy. San Diego has a Polish community large enough to support several Polish churches and civic organizations as well as an annual Polish festival. Perhaps Radek didn't find comfort in these reminders of home.

I listened, not saying much, simply enjoying looking at him. I thought to myself, Radek, I could make your time in the U.S. very happy. But I refrained from sharing my lascivious musings. I'm not in the habit of propositioning strangers, and a good appliance repair service is hard to come by.

As Radek knelt before my washer, he gazed up at me and asked, "Charnos (Charnas, my last name), this is Polish?"

"No. Close. It's Lithuanian," I replied, trying to sound neighborly. I wanted to create a bond with him, albeit a flimsy one, based solely on a shared border between the country he had left behind and the land of my ancestors.

Radek left for about an hour to pick up a needed part, and I used the time to walk up the street to a coffeehouse to buy a brownie . All that lust had induced a craving for sugar. The brownie was huge, so I ate half of it and wrapped up the other half. Radek returned but discovered he hadn't purchased the right part. He made plans to come back the next day after I got off work.

"You need to come back? What a shame!" (An outright lie.)

As he left the condo, I offered him the remainder of my brownie. Chocolate, after all, is the food of love, or in my case, lust.

The next evening, he arrived on time with the correct part for my machine. He told me he'd enjoyed the brownie. I asked how he was doing. He said he was feeling better, explaining that he hadn't been feeling well the day before. I told him I was feeling better too. He said I'd seemed sick the previous day.

I explained that I hadn't been sick; I'd been sad. An hour before he'd arrived, I learned that a twenty-three-year-old client, a favorite of mine, had died. Radek wanted to know about my work so I told him about my current and previous jobs working with the chronically ill and severely disabled. Describing my work is always good for impressing strangers. Most folks don't want to deal with the people I work with, and they think well of anyone who does.

He said, "You are very strong person."

I brushed off the compliment, but I was pleased I'd made an impact. I continued to schmooze him.

It turned out my washing machine repairman was a lover of independent films. He liked the movie *Unfaithful*, a sexy thriller starring Richard Gere and Diane Lane. This film was not independent, but I didn't say so. I told him I'd enjoyed it, too. He also had a passion for hang gliding in the desert.

He looked at me earnestly. "It's vat kips me alife."

I began to think of him as a moody, passionate type, kind of like Meryl Streep in *Sophie's Choice*, except without a tragic past or a suicide await-

15

ing him in his future. He said he rented a room and watched independent movies, alone, on cable late at night. He talked about how depressed he became when the wind didn't blow and he couldn't wind surf. I said I felt the same when I couldn't get to a movie.

To my surprise, our illusory "Old World" border bond appeared to be developing into something small but genuine. I still wanted to run my hands through his hair and down his chest, but I was also beginning to find this guy, up to his elbows in grease in front of my washer, truly interesting.

As he installed the new part, black sludge covered his hands. He needed rags to wipe them. I offered him my best ones. He apologized for using the rags, knowing they would be unsalvageable after he finished.

I dismissed the issue. "Don't worry—I have plenty!" Another lie, and I thought to myself, I'll have to buy new dust cloths for the antiques. Relinquishing the baby-soft rags was a gift to him. At this point, I think he might have started to catch on.

When Radek finished the repair, he stood over my bathroom sink, and I squirted soap from the dispenser into his hands, fully aware of the slightly seductive nature of my act. After he rinsed, I handed him towels in high handmaiden style. By now I was thoroughly enjoying myself.

When we completed the paperwork and I'd paid the bill, I left the apartment with him so I could throw a carton into the dumpster downstairs. Although he carried a heavy toolbox, Radek insisted on carrying the carton for me. On the elevator, he continued to tell me about himself.

When the elevator opened at the first floor, he said, "I am dive captain, too," as though he wanted me to know this last important fact about his life.

I never watched *Desperate Housewives*, but I gather that a hot young gardener loomed large in the plot. Now, post-encounter with Radek, I fully understand how otherwise reasonable women in their forties can find themselves lusting after younger, hunky men typically not considered romantic prospects.

I would never attempt seduction with my washing machine repairman. Yet, getting him to tell me about himself in a meaningful way was a seduction of sorts. I felt oddly satisfied that, in the space of two short meetings, he'd revealed some of his deepest feelings. His desire to tell me more, even as he was leaving, placed the cherry on top of my fantasy.

Who knows, maybe one day, if the wind isn't up in the desert and if he ever leaves his rented room, I may run into him at the movies. Or if my washer breaks again, maybe the repair service will send Radek back. A girl can dream.

Joanna J. Charnas

Chapter 4, 2005a

A DATE WITH BUDDHA

Was it something in the water? All week the staff had seemed anxious, impulsive, and mildly explosive. Professionals in a nursing home were not supposed to behave this way. By Friday, I believed the drama was over and I'd be able to work in peace. I was wrong.

I arrived on Ward B-3 to finish discharging a patient. It should have been a no-brainer. My job was to ensure that the forms I'd placed in the medical chart two days before were completed by the other various disciplines (Nursing, Occupational Therapy, Physical Therapy, Speech Therapy, etc.) and that the departing patient received her medications along with an explanation of how and when to take them. None of that had occurred. The nursing portion of the form was blank, and no one knew where the patient's medications were. In addition, no staff was available to complete the paperwork. And it only got worse from there. Voices were raised, frantic searches made, and generally unprofessional conduct was exhibited. I tried to remain calm and focused on completing the necessary tasks so our eager patient could be on her way. The last thing on my mind was romance.

So, when in my peripheral vision I saw a pair of deep-set, dark eyes looking at me and heard a voice say, "You have beautiful skin," I wasn't prepared. Nor was I prepared for what I saw when I turned my head and looked toward my admirer. A man dressed in the garb of a Buddhist monk—complete with maroon, floor-length robes, bare shoulders, and large wooden beads—gazed at me intensely. I thought I was staring at the

Buddha himself. My admirer looked at me soulfully. Not the way a Buddhist monk is supposed to look at a woman.

I have a rich and varied romantic history, but this was definitely a first. I could barely absorb it. The nursing staff still hadn't completed their tasks, and the chaos around me escalated. The nursing home medical director had informed me earlier in the week that I shouldn't discharge patients unless staff completed the forms in question, but no one on the ward knew anything about it. The charge nurse, whom I called on my office cell phone, refused to come to the ward to help.

I surmised that Buddha and his male companion, who stood next to him, were on the ward to visit a new patient. Less colorful than my admirer, the other guy looked like he was in his fifties and had dressed in khakis and a plaid button-down shirt. What, I wondered, were Buddha and Normal Guy doing together? Buddha and his buddy lingered in front of the nurse's station while the discharge turmoil played out. I may have exchanged small talk with him, but I'm not sure. When the discharge mess finally resolved, I left the ward and headed towards the administration building for a final sign-out, along with another social worker, Yaffa, who'd witnessed the pandemonium as well as my odd interaction with Buddha. Another colleague drove the patient to the administration building where we were meeting her.

As we walked down the long hall and out of the building, Yaffa observed, "That guy really liked you." Yaffa has killer instincts. She figures things out long before I do and is usually right. I'd sensed that familiar tingle from Buddha, but I couldn't quite believe it.

I replied weakly, "We did seem to make a connection." How could my admirer be a Buddhist monk? Are Buddhist monks allowed to have crushes? Are they allowed to date? I inquired, "What's the deal with the clothes?"

Yaffa replied, "He's a nice Jewish guy. He had a bar mitzvah. He's just seeking spirituality. The robes are a costume."

I asked her how she knew all this. Yaffa explained that earlier in the week, Buddha had been visiting a new patient and saw her nametag. He'd asked her about her last name and inquired if she was Jewish. Yaffa felt he had been drawn to her by her faith. They'd chatted a while, and she'd learned a little about him.

Buddha was drawn to Jewish women! Yaffa is married. She knows I'm Jewish. "My last name is a Hebrew acronym for the son-in-law of

Rabbi Nathan the scribe!" I exclaimed. "You can't get any more Jewish then that." But I remained befuddled.

Yaffa insisted. "We have to see him again."

She seemed upbeat, and her enthusiasm encouraged me. I began to believe I could develop the connections I'd sensed earlier.

Yaffa and I had seen Buddha, Normal Guy, and our new patient head into the nursing home chapel. I wasn't sure how we were going to crash their spiritual encounter, but Yaffa wanted to form a plan. I told her to let me think about it. In the meantime, we completed the final sign-out in the administration building and sent our discharged patient on her way home.

After the discharge, Yaffa and I headed back to the chapel. I hadn't yet figured out how to crash whatever was going on in there or what I would say when I saw my admirer again. When we arrived at the chapel, we stood in the vestibule for a few minutes, trying to decide how to proceed. By this time, we were both giddy. I told Yaffa I felt like a high school girl again. But high school was never this much fun. After thinking for a few minutes longer, I knew exactly what to say. I knocked on the chapel door and entered with Yaffa following me.

When I opened the door, Normal Guy knelt on the floor, rubbing the patient's feet. Buddha sat on the floor, eyes closed, apparently meditating. In our efforts to advance my love life, we'd interrupted some kind of healing ceremony. It looked heartfelt although somewhat funky. But our patient was critically ill and needed all the healing she could get. Who was I to judge?

I asked them to excuse our interruption and then launched into apologies for our visitors' exposure to the previous brouhaha. In full diplomatic mode, I stated that was not what we wanted visitors to experience. Buddha and Normal Guy were extremely gracious in return and assured us they hadn't been bothered. I managed to express something positive about the healing ceremony and offered my business card to both men "in case I can help in any way in the future." Buddha just happened to have a business card tucked deep in the folds of his robes. He whipped it out with lightning speed, and Normal Guy gave us cards, too. After a few more niceties, we shook hands with the two healers and departed. Buddha had a good, firm grip.

As soon as we exited the chapel, we regressed again into sixteen-year-olds. Yaffa called me "brilliant," and I soaked up her praise. I wondered to myself if my social work license could be revoked for such self-serving behavior. Yaffa and I agreed I had to finesse a first date with Buddha, and I decided I would ask him out for coffee. We tried to finish our workday in what continued to be full-moon-induced craziness.

Later, when I returned home, I took a closer look at Buddha's business card. It said his name was Lama Gensho, obviously not the name his parents lovingly bestowed upon him at birth. The card also said Gensho was a Buddhist priest. I had no idea what that meant or how it impacted my plan. If he was a lama and not a monk, did that change the rules? What were the guidelines for lamas? Were Buddhist priests like Catholic ones (no-love priests), or were they like Episcopalian ones (pro-love priests)? I had no idea.

According to his card, Lama/Priest Gensho lived in my neighborhood. What were the chances of that? I had an admirer who looked at me longingly, appreciated at least one of my physical attributes, and lived nearby. Unfortunately, a romance might be prohibited by religious restrictions. My goodness, this was complicated!

How did one gracefully ask out a lama/priest? I decided to focus on what I knew. I trusted Yaffa's instincts and perceptions. She was sharper than I was and probably smarter. I also knew that lama/priest or not, and whether he was supposed to or not, the guy liked me. Since I seemed to be squarely back in adolescence, I chose to play it cool and wait three days to give Gensho a call. All I faced was deep humiliation and embarrassment. What the hell.

The next morning, refreshed and in possession of a clearer head, I thought it wise to conduct some research before I did anything too stupid. I googled *Tibetan Buddhism* and read about the various levels of religious orders for Buddhist clergy. My reading material stated, unequivocally, that a vow of celibacy was part of the deal. That wasn't going to work at all.

On Saturday morning, I wanted to call Yaffa to consult with her about the snag in my plan, but as an observant Jew, she didn't answer her phone on Saturdays. I'd be on my own at least until sunset, when the Sabbath ended and she could use electronics again. I felt deflated and confused.

Being single was certainly becoming increasingly complicated. The men I met were too far away (my assessment), too old (their assessment), secretly attached to someone else (my assessment), having a mid-life crisis (their assessment), got cold feet for undeclared reasons (my assessment), or were simply not appropriate for an ever-expanding array of causes. When younger, I naïvely overlooked the obvious stumbling blocks in my romantic life. I made lots of mistakes and frequently had my heart broken, but I fell in love several times and had fun, too. Now the stumbling blocks I encountered couldn't blithely be ignored or bypassed. What to do? I put Gensho's business card in a drawer and went to the movies to distract myself.

The film helped me focus on matters besides my love life but only briefly. Sunset arrived, but I didn't have the heart to call Yaffa. Usually I can draw some kind of parallel to a movie, no matter what I encounter. I'd recently seen *Spring, Summer, Fall, Winter...and Spring*. In that film, a Buddhist acolyte develops a hearty lust for a pretty, young girl. The movie shows them fornicating in numerous lovely outdoor settings, including on a large rock (ouch). The acolyte leaves his isolated religious retreat to be with the girl but later returns, having murdered her in a crime of passion. That was not very helpful. I remembered seeing *Priest* in 1994. In that movie, the title character struggles with his earthly desires, but he's gay. Despite some universal themes, *Priest* was not going to cast enlightenment on my quandary. I'd also seen *The Third Miracle,* in which Anne Heche lusts after Ed Harris, a man of the cloth of the no-love variety. There's a big wallop of sexual tension between them, but Harris manages to resist her. I wanted to get the guy in my situation. Sadly, cinema was letting me down. I was on my own.

By Sunday, day two of my self-imposed three-day waiting period, I'd lost all my confidence. I talked to a friend and a family member about my encounter with Gensho. They were both supportive of my plan. I began to wonder what the parameters of celibacy were. I figured it definitely banned anything involving my fun parts. But did it rule out other kinds of touching? I cuddle with my cat, Zoe, every day, and we're definitely not having sex. Could I apply the same standards to a Buddhist priest? What were they allowed *to do*?

Were Buddhist priests permitted to have secular friends? I thought about the Dalai Lama. He had hung out with movie stars, so it made sense that Gensho could hang out with one middle-aged, divorced social worker. Finally, I realized I was overthinking the whole issue. You're supposed to do foolish things when you're a teenager, but the expiration date for this kind of behavior was at about twenty-five years old.

When Monday rolled around, one thing was certain; anyone who talked to me about my Buddhist fantasy would know in a flash that I wasn't a practicing Buddhist. I definitely was *not* living in the moment. I had tied myself in knots based on one compliment, a beaming smile, and my way-out-of-practice dating vibe. If I'd been a serene, centered Buddhist, I'd be calmer. Instead, I was living in dread of making a phone call to some nice Jewish guy who dressed strangely.

Sometime during a break from my insanity, I realized that in all of my dating experience, I'd never asked a man out. No wonder I was a wreck. Forty-five is not a great age to develop new and challenging dating skills. Throw in the uncertain religious element, and a case of the jitters made sense.

Fortunately, work is often my best therapy. By noon I felt like myself again. Yaffa and I went to lunch together, and I told her I'd decided to e-mail Gensho. E-mail would mitigate some of the awkwardness. Using e-mail seemed very un-lama/-priest like to me, but what did I know? I was glad to have an easier, less embarrassing means of communication than a phone call.

After lunch, with Yaffa as my editor, I wrote Gensho an e-mail that read something like this: "I enjoyed meeting you on Friday when you were visiting S. and felt we made a connection. I noticed the address on your business card is in my neighborhood. I would love to learn more about your work. Would you like to go out for coffee sometime?" Yaffa gave the message her seal of approval, and I took a deep breath and hit send. I felt so brave. Then, the waiting began.

Before I left work, I checked my e-mail. He hadn't responded. At seven that night, I checked again. Nada.

At 9:00 p.m., I checked once more, expecting the same result. Genuinely surprised, I found that he'd e-mailed me back and agreed to meeting. He gave me his home phone number, and I sent him a second e-mail saying I would call him the next day. Things were going more smoothly than I'd expected. Wow!

I called him after lunch the following day, disappointed to learn he'd recently moved and didn't live in my neighborhood anymore. But that wasn't a deal breaker. During our phone call, Gensho was funny and flirty. If I'd been arranging a blind date with him, I would never have guessed he was anything but a nice Jewish guy. We agreed to meet at a teashop that evening.

Our date was both strange and wonderful. It took only about ten minutes for me to learn, without much probing, that Gensho belonged to a sect of lamas permitted to have romantic relationships. Whew! All that worrying for nothing. The teashop had closed by the time we arrived so, instead, we ended up at a large, noisy, family-style pizza joint. I could barely hear so Gensho and I sat on the same side of our booth. This coziness allowed for some intense flirting. No rulebook existed for what to do on a first date with a lama/priest, and I still wasn't quite clear about the limits. I asked too many personal questions, and Gensho seemed nervous. By the time our date ended, I was exhausted but happy. At least one person stared at us although I barely noticed and didn't care. I hadn't felt this connected to anyone in years despite Gensho's unusual style of dress and religious lifestyle. We said goodbye while hugging and laughing. I smiled all the way home.

A few months earlier, I'd met someone who seemed like a good romantic prospect, but nothing developed between us. Since then the words that continuously ran through my mind, like a bad 1960's movie theme, were, "Do you remember love?"

I don't know whether there will be a second date with Gensho, but I'd like to see him again. During our date he was complimentary, extremely bright, and warm. He managed to be all those things despite my being tired and off-balance *and* despite his wearing what amounted to a dress. Gensho helped me remember viscerally all the best dates of my youth. I hadn't felt this good on a first date since my early thirties. So, whether or not we move forward, the answer to the question that's been haunting me for the last two months is this: Yes, I remember love.

Chapter 5, 2005b

SEQUEL: AN AFFAIR WITH BUDDHA

After three weeks of dating Lama Gensho, I found myself assessing the condom options in the Target pharmacy. Gensho had informed me he didn't like the Trojans that were tucked away in the back of my bathroom drawer, which we were using. He planned to go to Target to get the brand he preferred. What's not to love about Trojans, I wondered? They are the apple pie, the standard bearer, of all condoms. Not liking Trojans was like not liking the Yankees, but a guy had a right to use the prophylactic of his choice. I worked a couple of blocks from Target and offered to pick up the condoms for us at lunch. I asked him to dictate the brand and type he liked.

I remembered when we all started buying condoms religiously in the eighties. At first, my friends and I were nervous about it. We hadn't grown up expecting this to be part of our love lives, but we'd been compelled to overcome our inhibitions quickly. By the nineties, I bought condoms in the jumbo pack at Costco. I didn't give condom shopping at Target a second thought.

Gensho instructed me to buy the purple box but not the ribbed variety. Facing the rack of condoms at Target, I couldn't locate the purple box. Then I saw it, but it was the variety pack, which included the specifically unwanted ribbed type. During that time in my life, I hated using a cell phone and rarely turned mine on except when I traveled. I often found week-old messages on it and didn't even know the number by heart. But faced with confounding condom choices, I gave my lama a call.

"Gensho, I'm standing in the condom isle at Target, and the only purple box I can find is the variety pack." He laughed, and at his request I read out loud *all* of the descriptions on the four different boxes available in his chosen brand, complete with their special features. The condoms in the purple variety box contained features like *deep groove, extra deep groove, ribbed,* and something like *wild and wonderful.* We definitely didn't want the variety pack. Located directly below the condoms on the display rack were boxes of feminine de-itching goo. What looked like a mother-daughter combo approached the aisle, and the mom directed the younger one on what to buy. This necessitated her crouching below me and reaching around my legs in order to grab her desired product.

"Excuse me," she muttered.

"Oh, that's okay," I cheerfully replied. (People are so polite when they're buying things that they don't want to discuss at the dinner table.) Gensho and I continued to assess our options, and he finally asked me to purchase the gray box, which had lubricated condoms with no other special features.

Sometime during our second or third date, I had asked Gensho about his clothing. "Do you *ever* wear anything else?" I inquired.

"No" he answered, smiling at me.

"So, this is pretty much it for you?"

Busy adjusting his skirt, he barely looked up when he replied, "Yes."

In truth, the lovely egg-yolk color of his tunic showed off Gensho's beautiful olive skin, and the fabric was soft to touch. His lama uniform wasn't a problem for me, just interesting. People gave us second looks when we were in public together, but they didn't stare or make us uncomfortable. Besides, I think Gensho was inured to any kind of discomfort. He embraced his chosen lifestyle and was in his comfort zone, while I was completely unfamiliar with it. I tactfully pointed out to him that he'd been dating as a priest for some time, while being with him was my first romantic experience with clergy.

Gensho was funny, and he hadn't completely shaken off his Jewish upbringing. He peppered his conversations with Yiddish phrases, uttering things like, "Eat, Bubbela, eat," and "Do you need a nosh?" He signed off on e-mail with "Your Lama of love."

In many ways, dating Gensho felt like dating any other man. He liked boy movies, things with blood and action, and campy films. We went to the Cineplex and saw *Constantine,* a poorly written, semi-horror movie starring Keanu Reeves. It was about demons breaking through from Hell to the earthly world. We cringed at all the same moments and laughed at the same bad dialogue. Gensho saw about three seconds of *The Silence of the Lambs* as he channel-surfed and identified it immediately even though none of the leads were in the scene he'd glanced at. He may have dressed like the Dalai Lama, but in many ways, he was just a regular guy.

Slim and trim, Gensho could nevertheless wolf down larger volumes of food than I'd ever seen consumed outside of a casino buffet. He asked if he could say grace before we ate. I love grace and found the idea beautiful. However, the grace he recited seemed to go on for several minutes, and I worried about the food getting cold.

As for his religious beliefs, I allowed him to pray over my beloved cat, Zoe, who'd been ill recently. He held her, something she rarely allowed me to do. She purred during the prayer. She walked all over us and seemed to want his attention. Never having been a social creature, she'd only loved two people—an old friend of mine from Boston, whom she rarely saw, and me. I admitted to Gensho that not only did I have crush on him, but my cat did, too. It's one thing to charm a middle-aged woman coming out of a romantic dry spell. It's quite another thing to pull one over on a finicky geriatric cat.

At my request, he gave me another business card, and I carried it in my pocket for days until it became ragged. He'd offered to bless the card when he gave it to me, and I accepted. When the card began to disintegrate, I couldn't bear to throw it away. I finally zipped it into a pocket of my briefcase so I could carry it with me every day to and from work. I asked for several new cards and placed an unblessed one in my wallet, but the new one didn't feel the same.

Gensho asked to make plans with me two and three weeks in advance. While I tried to stay focused on whatever happy moment we were enjoying, he discouraged my "live in the moment" philosophy and encouraged me to think of our budding romance in terms of its long-term potential. He told me this is what he wanted and that I was the answer to his prayers.

I had every reason to think we were doing well. And we were, but then suddenly he changed, and we weren't.

On our first date after my jaunt to Target, Gensho hitched a ride with me after visiting our mutual patient, Sally, at the nursing home. He was deeply upset about his encounter with her. She suffered from end-stage AIDS and was declining rapidly. Gensho spent the entire half-hour ride home focused on his desire to heal her. He eventually asked permission to meditate in my car in order to center himself. Previously employed as an AIDS service provider for seven years, I knew all about this condition. I tried to be empathetic, but I felt drained when we reached my apartment. Not a good start to the pleasant evening I'd been looking forward to. He spent much of the rest of the night fixating on Sally, and he snapped at me. The shift in his behavior saddened me even after he apologized.

We hadn't established a level of intimacy that afforded him leeway to spend all our time together talking about *his* needs, desires, and fears. Gensho obsessed about his ability to heal Sally, but he hadn't learned one of the most important aspects of being a healer: do your best, and then let go. He appeared self-absorbed instead of patient-centered, and his desire to assist our mutual patient seemed less about healing Sally than about convincing himself he had the talents to do it. I was expecting a garden-variety date—I didn't know how to meet his sudden, unceasing neediness.

The following day, he cancelled our Friday night date two days in advance, stating he needed to catch up on sleep. When I confessed my disappointment and hurt, he invited me to his house to watch a DVD. When I arrived, he made me wait to watch the DVD while he clipped his toenails on his bedroom floor. When the movie was over, I went home so Gensho could sleep without distraction.

On our next date, Gensho spent much of the evening talking about a friend whom he'd just learned had received a disturbing medical diagnosis. All the lightness he'd brought to our relationship had dimmed. The mother of a childhood friend I'd grown up with was in hospice care, and I excused myself to make a ten-minute call to the friend. (His mother died the next day.) Gensho obsessed so much about *his* friend's bad news that he never asked me about the person in my life who was actually dying. It became apparent that once Gensho established a relationship, he used it as a means to meet his need for constant reassurance and support. Although happy to be supportive and reassuring, I couldn't focus on his needs every minute of our time together.

In addition, despite his gifts, I began to suspect that Gensho was a Buddhist priest in his mind only. He told me he didn't belong to an established Buddhist sect and that he was "a sect of one." He said he'd taken his vows to become a priest *esoterically,* and the local ashram despised him for reasons I didn't fully comprehend. All was not well in River City.

At the beginning of our relationship, Gensho had praised my linguistic flair, but he began correcting me during our final week together. I'd say something, and he'd reply, "Why don't you say . . . instead?" Or I'd begin to discuss a subject not having to do with us, and he'd respond, "I don't want to discuss that." He sometimes made assumptions about what I was going to say, which were often incorrect. It was a big change from where we'd started, when he'd delighted in my sense of humor and turn of phrase. I was suddenly in the presence of the Thought and Language Police.

When I met Gensho, I knew almost immediately that he had medical issues. At first, he seemed flexible about handling them, so I didn't mind. However, he became increasingly rigid. He stated he was a vegan, but he ate anything that appealed to him, with few exceptions. At one point, he asked me not to eat in front of him because non-vegan food was too tempting. He began to require long periods of time sitting bolt upright in order to digest his food comfortably, regardless of what he'd eaten. He'd changed.

Gensho assured me we could work out our differences, stating, "This is easy stuff."

I believed him, in large part because I wanted to. I knew the relationship wasn't going well, but the optimist in me hoped the changes were temporary. Gensho continued to be loving most of the time, and he expressed his appreciation of me in numerous ways.

I came home four days after receiving his assurances to a message asking me to phone him. When I called, he said he felt "icky." I asked why, and he responded that he didn't think "we should see each other romantically anymore." Although I inquired further as to why he wanted to break up, he would only say it was what his instincts told him to do. I asked for clarification, but he refused and urged me to also act on an instinctual level.

I agreed that we needed to break up. I have a very low tolerance for crankiness and wouldn't have put up with his much longer. But just that morning, Gensho had told me I was "a beautiful lover." I hadn't expected to end our relationship less than twelve hours later. I deserved more than his "instincts" as an explanation. He considered himself a follower of the Buddha of Compassion, but he seemed markedly lacking in any. He didn't acknowledge my feelings and instead asked if we could remain friends.

I inquired what he thought our friendship might look like. He wanted us to talk on the phone a few times a week and see each other about once a month. He left the ball in my court, inviting me to call him if I wanted to be his friend. I assumed Gensho had a history of dating women with extremely low self-esteem because I would never be his friend.

I needed a year and a half to heal from my divorce. Divorce was a world unto itself, and it had been a good twelve years since I'd experienced your run-of-the-mill break- up. Stunned by how much pain I felt, as usual, I searched for a movie reference to comfort me. I remembered Diane Keaton sobbing in *Something's Gotta Give* after her affair with Jack Nicholson ended. The affair lasted only a few days, but she sobbed long enough to write a play. I didn't feel as stupid about being heartbroken after thinking of her part in that movie.

I soothed myself by eating bad food, buying clothes I couldn't afford, and—my answer to all of life's ups and downs—going to the movies. Everything helped a little. Although hurt, I still missed the Gensho who'd courted me fiercely and made me feel loved. I have a high recidivism rate with my exes. Many of them have asked to get back together after we broke up even when *they* ended the relationships. I wondered if Gensho would call me and was deeply relieved when he didn't. I knew it was better to let go. I just felt lousy.

I planned to make a concrete effort to move on. I considered going on Jewishfriendfinder.com on the Internet, but my vacation started in three weeks, I didn't want to lose a week of a month-long membership so it seemed wiser to wait to join after the vacation.

Almost a week into the breakup, I saw a good-looking man smiling at me from his vintage white Corvette, and I felt I still had the goods to meet someone new. I was getting better.

Gensho had spent his first night in my home sleeping on the side of my bed where Zoe slept. She favored the upper left-hand corner of the mattress. When I suggested we switch sides to accommodate her, he'd stated he "loved" that side so I didn't push the issue even though Zoe abandoned the bed whenever he slept over. After he dumped me, Zoe returned to her customary place. She became more affectionate than usual as if to indicate approval that our lives were back to normal. I told her I agreed with her.

I'm glad I had the affair with Lama Gensho, whose legal name, I learned, was Darren Schwartzman. Even though things went downhill rapidly, and being abruptly dumped hurt me, we had several great weeks. He couldn't sustain a relationship because of his overwhelming needs, but I believe his initial affection and respect for me were genuine. Feeling that again was wonderful.

I'm hoping that between my numerous crushes and an actual affair some forward momentum will enter my love life. I feel positive about the way things are heading. Maybe the next time someone stares at me in stalled traffic from his Corvette, he'll ask for my phone number. Or maybe I'll ask for his.

SAM: ACTING AS IF

I've always contended that God has a sense of humor. In a rational world, how else can the duckbilled platypus or Devo's top-forty hit be explained? My conviction was confirmed when I received a phone call from Sam.

Sam. The name seemed so innocuous. It's the name of the guy who's tutoring your kid in algebra or of your big brother's best friend. Show's what I know.

After Darren Schwartzman, aka Lama Gensho, dumped me, I sensed a void in my life that hadn't existed before dating him. He'd been such an intense presence, albeit a brief one, that when he abruptly exited my life, I felt his absence keenly. Even after mourning our relationship, I wasn't the same as I'd been prior to our month-long romance. I'd been at peace with my private life before the affair. Now, I was restless.

I thought a little hair-of-the-dog might be a good antidote to my unsettled feelings. I needed to get out of the house and go on a date. I'd tried different methods of meeting men since my divorce, and none had been successful. I'd had particularly bad luck with Internet dating services and didn't want to throw away my money again. The sites produced only a few dates, and I hadn't clicked with any of the guys I'd met through them. All the men with whom I'd connected in any meaningful way post-divorce, I'd met spontaneously. Then, my ex-husband and another friend suggested I try using Craigslist's personal ads. (This was several years before the infamous Craigslist Killer murdered a masseuse after answering her Craigslist ad, turning people off to meeting singles through the site.) Despite my disappointing Internet forays, I thought I'd give it another try. At least, it was free.

The first week I ventured onto Craigslist, I managed to engage three men in a bit of Internet chat. One of them decided I was too old. Another dropped into Cyber-oblivion after he received my photograph. The third one called me but never actually asked me out. About a week after our phone call, he sent me an e-mail that said, "Do you like me?" I replied that I did, but then I never heard from him again. This was not going any better than last time around.

I went on vacation and took a break from all thoughts of dating. When I came home, I decided to keep trying. I thought I'd cruise through Craigslist personals once a week to see if there was anyone whom a recently dumped forty-five-year-old might conceivably date.

The first week after my vacation, I replied to an ad but never received a response. My Internet curse appeared to be alive and thriving. I wondered why I bothered at all. The second week, Sam's ad caught my eye. He wrote that he'd recently moved from Seattle and wanted to meet women with whom he could go to concerts, movies, and dinner. He was interested in finding either a friend or a romantic partner. He sounded appealingly down to earth. We traded a few pleasant e-mails, and he wrote that he wanted to get together. He didn't ask to see my photograph—a first. I gave him my phone number and wondered if he, too, would drop into the cyber-void.

A couple of days later, my phone rang. A heavily accented male voice asked for me. He didn't sound like the usual brand of telemarketers, who never seem able to pronounce either my last *or* first name. When he introduced himself as Sam, my response, which I uttered without a second thought, was "Sam, you have an accent." He must have thought he was talking to the village idiot. Sam conceded that he did. I asked him where he was from.

"Persia," he replied. Persia, as in Iran, as in possibly Muslim. OH, NO! No, no, no, no, no, no, no! He must have heard the hesitancy in my voice because he asked, "Is that all right?"

I replied, "Sure, if it's okay that I'm Jewish." This is how I know I will never have a second career in international diplomacy. I can easily talk to people who are floridly psychotic or comfort patients' families who are going through the most life-wrenching experiences, but I apparently cannot gracefully handle a little surprise involving cross-cultural dating.

I had envisioned Sam as an earthy, possibly dirty blond, backpacking type. I'd gone to college near Seattle, and I'd met dozens of men like that. I was not prepared for an Iranian. As Sam and I made first-contact small talk, I let my mind wander. If he and I hit it off, I wondered how my family would react to me dating someone from the Middle East. They were still puzzling out my romance with someone who dressed like a Buddhist monk. (The most frequently asked question: "Did it bother you that he dressed *like that*?" No, it honestly hadn't bothered me at all.) How much worse could an Iranian be? I was reminded of the cultural conflicts in *Mississippi Masala*, a movie in which a young and hunky Denzel Washington falls in love with a woman from India by way of Uganda. Her family has a major meltdown over their affair. It wasn't the quite the same situation, but thinking about it didn't reassure me. I tried to give my nearest and dearest some credit for being openminded. They are all warm, liberal people. They want me to be happy. If I was happy, they might be okay with an Iranian. Or maybe not. I wasn't sure. I refocused on the call, reminding myself I had to get through a first date before worrying about family condemnation.

Sam started the phone call by establishing the time and place for our date. He immediately won points by eliminating all the awkwardness of waiting to find out if we liked each other enough to meet by promptly taking the plunge and committing to a rendezvous. He told me he had black hair. In order to make it easy for me to find him in the coffee shop where we would meet, he said he'd be wearing a black shirt and black pants.

"Great," I thought, "He's going to look like a terrorist." I wondered how I got myself into this.

But when Sam told me he read nonfiction because he wanted to learn new things, he scored more points than I'd expected. I like an inquisitive mind. We talked about movies and discovered we'd both enjoyed the same independent film. Sam and I discussed whether Sean Penn had received his Oscar for the correct performance. We agreed that Sean had been even better in *21 Grams* than in *Mystic River*, for which he won the award. We concurred that he'd been a shoo-in the year he won, based on his twenty-plus years of superlative acting. I love the Academy Awards and decided that anyone I could discuss the Oscars with deserved a chance, with or without millennia of ethnic warfare marking our present and ancestral histories.

My date with Sam turned out to be quite pleasant. He was attractive, and he engaged me in interesting conversation. Sam seemed open, and he talked about his desire to start his own business (a small franchise of some sort) and his religious beliefs (born Muslim but not practicing). He quoted Einstein without seeming pretentious. He laughed easily, and I felt comfortable with him. After about two hours of relaxed chatting, we ran out of things to say, which seemed fine to me, in the absence of any activity to anchor our conversation.

Yet, despite its pleasantness, the date had none of the sizzle and pop I'd felt with Darren Schwartzman/Lama Gensho, nor did I feel the connection or flirtiness I'd had right away with him. I sensed that Sam was lonely, although he didn't say so. This was serious business for him, not fun and games. I reminded myself afterward that taking things slowly was much healthier than jumping feet first into the deep end of the pool as I had done recently. Comparing anyone to Lama Gensho, who I was beginning to think of as a nut, was unfair.

I left the date having no idea if I would ever hear from Sam again. I'd had countless first dates like this one. Sometimes the guy called; sometimes he didn't. There was no way to tell. Part of me wanted to see Sam again, just for the get-out-of-house-with-a-nice-straight-man factor, and part of me didn't care. I hadn't felt enough of a connection to him to be disappointed, and that came as a relief after caring so much about someone else just a short time ago.

A week later, I still hadn't heard from Sam and assumed I probably wouldn't. This was okay with me. I was glad I had gone on a date, any date, with someone reasonably sincere and sane. However, although I hated to admit it, after the date with Sam, I still felt as though there was a small crater in my soul that Darren Schwartzman/Lama Gensho had left, nut or not. But I also thought of the great Alcoholics Anonymous aphorism, "Act as if." At least, I'd done that. I'd gone through the motions of moving on and was proud of myself. If my heart wasn't quite in it yet, my intentions were. I was going to keep trying.

LET'S BE FRIENDS

There are still many things I don't understand about men. Lately, I've been puzzling over failed romantic prospects who wanted to become my friends. In the past six months, three romantic rejects asked me to befriend them, two of whom I met on blind dates and one, Darren Schwartzman/Lama Gensho, with whom I had a full-fledged, swinging-from-the-chandelier affair. I believe the offers of friendship were sincere, not cop-outs to mitigate the sting of rejection, theirs or mine, but I didn't want to be friends with any of them.

If you reject me romantically, or if I don't like you enough to give you a shot at winning my heart, chances are I won't want to be your friend. And if you break my heart, I'm more likely to engage in creative visualizations involving pushing you off a cliff than I am to enjoy a casual dinner with you now and then. The idea of staying friends post-rejection seems deeply unsatisfying.

Remaining friends with your ex makes sense if you're in school, often because it's the sanest, most diplomatic course of action. If you're going to see someone daily in Biology 101, or if you hang out with the same social group as your ex or live down the hall in the dorm, it behooves you to at least be friendly, if not actual friends. Otherwise, life is going to be unpleasant for everyone. But for middle-aged women like me with busy schedules and satisfying lives, I'm not sure what the point is of becoming friends post-rejection.

I posed this question to my big brother, Charles. He suggested that if I reject a man, he might think I'll change my mind if he sticks around in the guise of friendship. I told Charles his theory might apply to the men I rejected, but it didn't explain the men who rejected me. Despite his usual fount of big brother good advice and wisdom, Charles didn't have any additional insights on the matter. He, too, was stumped.

I didn't always embrace my no-friendship philosophy. When I was younger, more open, and generally more stupid, I allowed myself to be friends with both the rejected *and* the rejecters. At twenty-three, I became friends with Al. He and I met at a singles event. Only three people attended the function—Al, his friend, and me. We met in a casual, well-lit bar in downtown Palo Alto. Al's friend departed after an hour, and Al suggested he and I make an evening of it together. Even though the event was a non-starter, I'd psyched myself up for a night out, hoisted on my pantyhose, and arrived promptly on time. So, I figured, why not? This was in 1983, just as Silicon Valley was emerging and Palo Alto was still fundamentally a college town. Al and I took a long, pleasant walk along the main drag and got acquainted. A couple of years older than I, Al worked as a young professional in an unmemorable business capacity. He was smart and nice enough. On paper, we should have been a perfect match, but at twenty-five, Al already looked middle aged. His demeanor was sodden as if burdened by the concerns of a man twice his age. He didn't have even a smidgen of *joie de vivre* or sex appeal.

Al made it clear he wanted to become romantically involved, and I made it equally clear I wasn't interested. Although rejected, he still wanted to be my friend. So, for about a year and a half until he left the Bay Area, I'd see him once in a while. Al never fully accepted my rejection, and he periodically asked to review the reasons I wouldn't give him a chance. Each time he brought up the issue, I'd patiently explain the truth: that special something just wasn't there for me, but his nagging quickly got old.

Eventually, Al moved to Los Angeles, then several months later came back for a visit. At his request, I allowed him to camp out in my living room for a few days. This must have been a special kind of torture for him although one of his own choosing. During the visit, he asked me to photograph him in his Speedo, saying he wanted to see what he looked like in it. Instead of replying, "Baby doll, go look in a mirror if you want to see what you look like in your bathing suit," I obliged and took the pictures. I understood that the photo session was really an opportunity for me to see him as scantily clad as I'd allow. Turned out he looked pretty good in his Speedo. But whatever his fantasy, it didn't materialize. I never changed my mind. Several months later, he met a girl and proposed within a couple of weeks of their first date. He disappeared from my life shortly thereafter.

In another youthful interlude, I met Zach on a blind date after answering his personal ad. Zach was forty, and I was thirty at the time. I knew almost immediately that he had no romantic interest in me. He never said so explicitly, but I could tell. Zach also made it clear he wanted to be friends. He was charming, smart, and funny. As a critic for the *Boston Phoenix*, the local alternative newspaper, Zach received free tickets to cultural events. His ad didn't produce the girl of his dreams, but he and I shared a zippy energy that had us going out frequently to movies and theater. We attended a preview of *Pretty Woman* and saw a road show of A.R. Gurney's *Love Letters*, starring the late greats, Jason Robards and Elaine Stritch. Zach was an astute critic, and he always engaged me in thought-provoking conversation after we watched a play or movie. We had intimate phone conversations lasting hours, and by the fourth month of our friendship, I began to feel as though we were having a platonic affair. It reminded me of the relationship between Meg Ryan and Billy Crystal in *When Harry Met Sally* before they slept together and complicated matters. Zach and I became so close that the reality of our emotional intimacy and concurrent lack of physical intimacy began to feel uncomfortably disjointed. I struggled with the issue and finally decided to be brave and ask Zach why he'd vetoed romance with me. Zach handled what might have been a painful conversation with delicacy and used the classic answer: he didn't "feel any chemistry" with me. Hard to believe, but at thirty, I'd never heard this before. I knew what he meant, though, and I was satisfied with his answer.

We'd met in February, and by mid-summer Zach had become involved with a baker who fed him day-old baked goods and doted on him. By Labor Day, I'd begun dating someone who kept me preoccupied all fall. Zach and I continued to see each other, but things slowed down. By the following fall, we'd faded from each other's lives with no hard feelings. Zach was fun for a long time, and my youthful perplexity didn't detract from enjoying his friendship.

In retrospect, my friendships with Zach and Al were relationships of young adulthood. They weren't necessarily mistakes, but they don't bear repeating. They helped me figure out what I needed and what I didn't want in the future.

I have one ex-boyfriend with whom I stayed friends for years, but the circumstances were unusual. Andy was the son of an old friend of my mother's, and I'd known him, or about him, through our mothers my whole life. We hadn't been friends before we began dating, but he was a familiar entity. Although disappointed, I felt fine about continuing to socialize with him casually after he decided he didn't want to date me any longer. Andy and I married other people within three months of each other, and six years after his romantic rejection, we were guests at each other's weddings.

Given the right circumstances, I might still be willing to be friends with former romantic prospects or even people I've slept with. But starting a friendship post-rejection with a virtual stranger, after one date, or with someone who's dumped me doesn't appeal to me or make much sense.

Jake, the first in the recent string of men seeking my friendship, stood the best chance of becoming my friend. He was a decent person, just confused. A mutual pal set us up. We took a long walk on the beach on Coronado Island to the world-famous Hotel del Coronado, where *Some Like It Hot* was filmed. At the hotel, we bought coffee and sipped it slowly on our walk back up the beach. At the end of the date, Jake asked if he could hug me goodbye, and he embraced me so intensely, a stranger might have thought he was sending me off to war instead of dropping me off in front of my condo. Jake said he wanted to see me again and told me he would call.

I know I'm old fashioned, but I still adhere to the three-day rule: If a man wants a second date, barring national catastrophe, medical crisis, or death in the family, he'll contact me within three days after the first date. So, by the fourth day, I knew matters wouldn't proceed smoothly. Saying "I'll call you" means nothing in man-speak. Guys might as well be telling you they have a dental appointment. But our mutual friend assured me of Jake's sincerity, so I continued to wait to hear from him instead of assuming the jig was up as I would have with anyone else.

Sure enough, on day five Jake telephoned. He explained he'd been thinking about our date. He gave me a brief sketch of his relationship history, which included a recent breakup. Ultimately, he declared he was having a mid-life crisis and had decided since our date that he didn't want to see anyone for a while. It didn't sound like an excuse when he said he liked me and wanted to hang out with me occasionally and attend movies together. I think I surprised him when I said I needed to know if he was tactfully trying to tell me he didn't find me attractive because in that case, I wasn't interested. I didn't want a repeat of my friendship with Zach.

"No," he said, "I just need some time to focus on myself." He added that he wanted to be relationship free. In this particular case, I was willing to inhabit some relaxed gray zone and enjoy it without expectations.

A couple of weeks later, Jake called to arrange a get-together and said he wanted to "revisit" our previous conversation. He was concerned that while we were hanging out, I'd be waiting for him to change his mind about getting involved with me—Charles's theory. Except Jake seemed to have forgotten that he was the one who'd wanted just to hang out with me, not the other way around. I repeated what I told him during our previous conversation and added that I didn't want to spend time together and later find out he'd become involved with someone else. I explained that doing so would hurt my feelings.

"Well, that might happen," Jake replied. He then chose to tell me he didn't feel any chemistry with me, and I informed him I didn't want to socialize with him. Jake went from asking me out to asking me to hang out to saying he'd never had any romantic interest in me. I decided he'd been right; he *was* having a mid-life crisis. He didn't know what he wanted. I hoped he could sort himself out, but it wasn't going to be at my expense.

Substituting my morning cup of coffee for a tall glass of Tabasco sauce was more likely than ever becoming Darren Schwartzman/Lama Gensho's friend. Perhaps other former flames had agreed to be friends with him, but I never for a second considered it. I find it hard to believe he thought I would ever be his friend. I don't socialize with people who callously dump me.

I feel bad for the third in my recent string of men who sought my friendship. He was a good person and deserved to find a nice woman to love him; it just wasn't going to be me. I met Tommy on another blind date. Within five seconds of our meeting, I knew I was never going to find him physically attractive. I spent two hours schmoozing and trying to get to know him over coffee in a local coffee shop, but I never felt connected. At the end of the date, as I was about to get into my car, he asked me if I wanted to see him again. I told him the truth—I hadn't felt any chemistry with him. (Thank you, Zach.) Tommy stated he felt chemistry could develop over time. He argued he'd recently dated a woman with whom he'd had great chemistry, but it had burned out. I wasn't sure of the point of his argument. That chemistry was ephemeral? But his earnestness moved me and caught me off guard. In my moment of weakness, I agreed to a second date. Tommy hopped into his Mercedes a happy guy.

I knew immediately that I'd made a mistake. I received a sweet e-mail from him the next morning, praising my virtues. He wrote something about "at least making a new friend." He assumed friendship was a given, regardless of what transpired romantically. I read the e-mail quickly and with increasing horror but avoided responding to him all day.

By late afternoon, I couldn't bear the dread any longer. I wrote him back, detailing all the ways I feel chemistry—physically, emotionally, intellectually, or spiritually—but hadn't felt it at all with him. Wincing as I typed, I told him I didn't want to see him again. I explained that I was looking for romance, not friendship, and apologized for being ambivalent or accidentally hurting his feelings. Then, I wallowed in Jewish guilt for the rest of the evening. Tommy was a prince and didn't add to my misery by replying to my e-mail.

Last summer at a low point, I made a list of all the men not related to me who love me, and I called it "The Eight Men Who Love Me." In addition to the men on the list, there are a few others who don't necessarily love me but with whom I have warm relationships. I feel fortunate to have these guys in my life. Our relationships aren't substitutes for something else. It's not like there was no butter in the house so I just used canola oil instead. My friendships don't work that way. In most cases, I met my friends in school or at work. I was genuinely surprised and touched when several of the relationships survived their original, easy-access environments. My friendships aren't consolation prizes for something desired that didn't transpire. They are heartfelt endeavors.

Maybe my aversion to friendship with romantic duds makes me an old stick-in-the-mud, but I don't want to treat friendship like a second-rate substitute for a preferred outcome. There are a host of movies about men and women who have adult friendships, but almost all of them involve unresolved sexual tension—the most famous being *When Harry Met Sally*—or depict relationships in which at least one of the friends is gay, as in *My Best Friend's Wedding*. Some of these friendships revolve around work. I don't think I've ever seen a film depicting straight, adult, single men and women who started as friends as remain friends. This realization helps me value my male friends deeply. I'm fortunate to have them. Friendship, with all genders, ought to evolve because something lovely, delightful, or intellectually stimulating occurs between two people. Otherwise, why bother? My friends, I'm sure, would all agree.

THE SAFETY DOLLAR

I recently remembered a small tidbit from my childhood that I hadn't thought of in decades: the safety dollar. In the 1960s, my brother Charles and I lived in New York City on the Upper East Side. By 1968, both of us were allowed, even when alone, to navigate the area of the city surrounding Central Park. When I visit New York now, I'm surprised my parents allowed me to walk around the city by myself at eight years old, but it was a different world then. Children were more independent in many ways than children are now. I wasn't the only kid walking home alone from school by the end of second grade. Our mother gave both my brother and me a "safety dollar." The safety dollar was there to help us if we ever encountered an emergency. I'm not sure exactly what Mom intended. A dollar was enough money to pay bus fare if we lost our bus passes or to make numerous emergency phone calls, but the safety dollar wouldn't have been sufficient to rescue us from a larger crisis. For example, it wouldn't have paid for a cross-town taxi. I assume Mom wanted assurances that if Charles or I got stuck in a small way, we'd have some assistance available.

I've begun to think of my crush on Henry Cooper as the romantic equivalent of the safety dollar. It's never going to evolve into a relationship, but it serves as a source of genuine comfort. It confirms that I'm still capable of ardent feelings and reminds me that the dim pilot light fueling my romances has not been extinguished from either lack of use or misuse. My crush has both amused and succored me since I first met Henry.

I saw Henry again this year when I returned to New York for my annual spring visit. Last year, I'd seen Henry several times when my father stayed with him during our concurrent visits to New York. This time both my father and stepmother, Suzy, were in the city for Passover and the yearly family Seder. They stayed at the *pied-à-terre* of a friend instead of at a hotel. Dad told me he'd be visiting Henry and invited me to join my stepmother and him for lunch with them.

The previous summer, I'd outed my crush to my parents, and I'd spent the following nine months making joking references to it. I didn't know what an actual face-to-face with Henry in my parents' presence might be like. My father, however, can be extremely gracious, and I felt confident that he and my stepmother would not embarrass me. Still, I worried that I'd feel self-conscious or uncomfortable because of my own emotions. After some internal debate, my fondness for Henry overrode my concerns about any discomfort I might experience, and I decided to accept their invitation.

Henry seemed to have a gift for picking wonderful dining spots. Last year, we'd eaten at the Trustee's Dining Room in the Metropolitan Museum of Art. This year, he selected the newly refurbished Algonquin Hotel in the New York Theater District, site of the famous writers' roundtable of the nineteen twenties.

When I arrived for lunch, Dad, Suzy, and Henry had already been seated. Henry rose to shake my hand as I entered the dining room. Not many men do that anymore, and the sparks of my crush immediately reignited. At the beginning of our lunch, Henry called me Pat several times. Pat is my mother's name. She died in 1986, and my father and she separated almost forty years ago. I could hardly hold the name mishap against him, though. My grandmother often called me Pat after enjoying a couple of evening cocktails.

Henry had informed Dad and me last year that he'd performed a small role in the movie, *The Life Aquatic with Steve Zissou.* He'd acquired his role through one of his three daughters who was employed in the film industry and worked on the movie. His part consisted of about five seconds of face time and two lines. I teased Henry about being a movie star, and he replied, "Yes, I am." I asked him if he'd become a member of the Screen Actors Guild and received his SAG card. We enjoyed a brief exchange about whether or not he'd chosen to sign up for their health benefits, a silly conversation given that Henry lives on Fifth Avenue and clearly does not need group health coverage through his new union membership.

During most of the lunch, Dad and Henry discussed their mutual friends, and Henry asked polite questions about what my father and step-mother had been up to during the past year. Much of this conversation focused on an old high-school classmate who'd dropped out of the world they'd been groomed for at prep school and who was living in a single-room-occupancy hotel in Texas. Both Dad and Henry spoke with affection and concern for this friend. He enjoyed receiving postcards, and Dad lamented that since he'd begun to write his grandchildren regularly, he was sending less mail to the classmate. In the middle of the conversation, Henry sprang from the table and soon returned with three blank post-cards, which he planned to mail after lunch. Each of us contributed even though I'd never met this friend. I wrote, *Having a great lunch with Dad, Suzy, and Henry. Regards, Jo Charnas.* I was glad to be a part of the effort.

As the discussion progressed, the depth of care Dad and Henry expressed for their friend touched me. They seemed to feel a sense of responsibility for him even though their connection to him was five decades old. My crush instantly evolved from a silly conceit to sincere respect for Henry. I was proud of my father, too, for his decency and desire to be kind to someone who'd once had a promising future but had been unable to realize the potential both Dad and Henry manifested in their lives.

The food at the Algonquin was delicious. I sat at the table, enjoying my tomato and mozzarella salad, letting the conversation ripple around me. I imagined Dorothy Parker sitting in the same seat, drinking too much and exchanging clever repartee with other members of the Round Table. Remembering the movie, *Mrs. Parker and the Vicious Circle*, starring Jennifer Jason Leigh, made this easier to envision. The scenes of the Algonquin are full of smart and lively banter. But despite their great talents, I couldn't imagine any of the members of the Round Table, icons of early twentieth-century literature, being more charming and erudite than Henry, the man sitting right next to me.

Toward the end of lunch, Henry commented on the Michael Jackson child molestation trial, which was in its middle stages. Suzy stated that in order to follow the trial, you needed to watch the television coverage. I countered that I was reading about the trial every day in the newspaper. I like to read the paper at work while I eat lunch. This perked Henry up, and he wanted to know my thoughts about Michael Jackson. Like many people of my generation, I'd grown up with Michael Jackson's music and loved the early Jackson Five recordings. I'd been captivated by the great songs on *Thriller*, Michael Jackson's mega-hit album of the early eighties. I delivered a brief history of Michael Jackson's music and my psychosocial assessment of the artist since the mid-eighties, when the King of Pop stopped making super-successful albums and became increasingly peculiar. Henry appeared keenly interested and asked insightful questions. My parents, of course, couldn't participate in this conversation at all, so for about ten delightful minutes, I held Henry's full attention.

As the meal ended, both Dad and Henry commented on what a great time they'd had. They said "we" should do this every year. I'm fairly certain I wasn't necessarily part of the "we," but I was glad I'd been included that day. And by the end of the meal, Henry was calling me by my correct name. As he departed for an appointment, he kissed me goodbye on the cheek.

After Henry left, Dad, Suzy, and I lingered in the Algonquin lounge. Dad praised my poise and seemed impressed by my discourse with Henry about Michael Jackson. But I give Dad and Suzy most of the credit for how relaxed I felt. If we were not the kind of family we are, I'd never have agreed to join them for lunch after admitting my thing for Henry. I trusted they would never do anything to make me uncomfortable, and they didn't. They'd put me at ease, which helped me process my feelings for Henry during the lunch.

After the three of us separated for the afternoon, I walked around the city and thought about what had changed since I was first taken with Henry Cooper. Although still smitten, my fondness had deepened. He was as sophisticated and amusing as I remembered, but he'd shown a depth of kindness, demonstrated by concern for his old friend, that I hadn't had an opportunity to witness the previous year.

I still find everything about Henry completely charming. I love his messy hair and his super-WASP accent. I love that after our brief discussion last year on the merits of tweed, he'd actually worn a snazzy tweed jacket to our lunch at the Algonquin. But more than anything, I love having him in the background of my consciousness, and I cherish the little glow I get every time I think of him. Like the safety dollar of my childhood, my crush on Henry gives me a small measure of comfort. It's a freestanding entity that doesn't interfere with my openness for a real relationship. Instead, it simply remains what it's always been—a sweet, sweet thing.

FUN AND GAMES

I recently asked Tantra Puja, the organization that holds tantric sex workshops in San Diego, to remove me from their e-mail list. Without my knowledge, Darren Schwartzman/Lama Gensho gave my e-mail address to them so I held him responsible for the cheerful messages about their activities I'd received over the previous two months. Before L.G. dumped me, he'd asked me to attend a tantric workshop with him. He'd explained workshop participants remained clothed and no actual sex was performed. I agreed to attend with the caveat that I'd only participate in the exercises with him. I didn't want to be touched by strangers. I'd been curious about what took place at the workshops and disappointed that we broke up before I had a chance to find out.

But post-breakup, the e-mails unnerved me. I was trying to get over Lama Gensho, and Tantra Puja wasn't helping. However, I'd be lying if I pretended not to be oddly fascinated. The first e-mail described a workshop similar to the one I'd signed up for. I read it to see if I could find out more about what I'd missed, but I didn't learn much. The second described a tantric support group. I wondered why a support group was needed in order to practice tantric sex. If Sting talked about it on Oprah, how tough could it be? There were several more announcements regarding the group, which discussed whether it would be open or closed, its future direction, etc. Aside from the subject matter, the group seemed fairly mundane. Then, I received an e-mail about a third workshop. This announcement stated it would include dancing at sunset (or maybe sunrise) and partial nudity, but again, no sex. This invoked images of 1960s hippies, like the ones in the commune scene from the classic film, *Easy Rider.* I hadn't liked the movie, and remembering it brought to mind scraggly looking folks in earth-tone colored clothes badly in need of laundering. I can understand the value of learning ancient techniques in order to gain greater personal fulfillment. I cannot understand why anyone would want to dance partially nude with strangers in bad light. I wrote to Tantra Puja saying I'd enjoyed receiving their announcements but that an old boyfriend had placed me on the e-mail list and I wished to be taken off. I haven't heard back from them, and I'm hoping that last e-mail will be their final message.

The same week I tried to purge myself of the Tantra Puja's e-mails, I saw something in the window of the Crypt, my local sex emporium, which caught my attention. It was a sign that read, "All handcuffs twenty-five percent off!" The Crypt is located two blocks from my home. I pass it every day on my way to and from work, and I've become inured to its existence in the neighborhood.

This time, the sign sparked my imagination. I wondered how much street traffic the announcement brought in. If you weren't thinking about replacing your current set of handcuffs, did the sale announcement inspire you to buy a shiny or furry new pair? If you'd never used handcuffs as part of sex play, did it convince you to buy your first pair? The Crypt is located on the corner of a major thoroughfare about a mile north of the world-famous San Diego Zoo. I envisioned some sweet midwestern couple, on their way to the zoo, spotting the handcuffs-on-sale sign. Perhaps the wife (the one I identify with) asked her husband if they could "stop *there* on our way back to the hotel." The new sex toy might add unexpected excitement to their vacation.

Between the exotic messages from the tantric folks and the sign at the Crypt luring more adventuresome people than me onto their premises, I began to feel boring. Boring *and* boyfriend-less, a bad combination. I've never found sex toys alluring. The closest I'd been to bondage and discipline was watching *9 ½ Weeks*, a movie that wasn't sufficiently kinky to receive an X rating. I felt pathetic, and it got me thinking.

I suppose the nearest I ever came to anything kinky was with Ezra Cohen. It hadn't been one of my finest moments as a human being, not because of the sexual issue, but because of my dishonesty.

I met Ezra over Memorial Day weekend when I was twenty-four, and I dated him until the end of August. Of all my romantic experiences, the three-month relationship with him was the most casual. My heart hadn't been in it. Ezra was forty years old, and we were at different stages in our lives. We met once or at most twice a week and usually stayed in, cooking dinner for each other, watching television, and talking.

Sometime shortly after our relationship became intimate, he told me he wanted to have a threesome with me and another woman. There was no way on God's great earth I was participating in a threesome, but I knew that a threesome was the archetypical straight-male fantasy. So, in order to give Ezra the pleasure of a good fantasy, I made the following deal: I would round up another women for a threesome if first we had a threesome with a man. Part of the deal was that Ezra had to find the second man.

Everything I knew about Ezra indicated he stood on the far hetero side of the Kinsey scale. Assured that a threesome with him and another man wasn't going to take place, I believed I'd never be asked to uphold my end of the bargain. As expected, sometime in mid-August, Ezra informed me that he'd tried to find a man for our threesome but was having second thoughts about the matter.

"No problem," I replied. "I understand." I was so nice about it. Shame on me; I lied. If there's a special place in Hell for disingenuous girlfriends, I'll be doing some time there in the hereafter.

A few years later, I made my second foray into all things kinky with Dan, who needed to buy a sex aid. Dan is my oldest friend. We met in nursery school when we were both three. In the fall of 1986, I'd moved to Boston to attend graduate school. Through a quirk of fate, Dan was also in Boston that year, attending classes at the same university. My boyfriend of two years and I had broken up mid-fall, and I was still recovering from the sudden death of my mother earlier that year. Although I was making new friends in school, Dan was the only person in town who knew me well.

One night, feeling particularly blue, I gave Dan a call and asked him if we could hang out. Dan declined, stating he had to run an errand but invited me come along. He explained, without so much as a pause, that he needed to buy a cock ring for an ex- girlfriend. That statement immediately jerked me out of my morose mindset. Why, I queried, did he need to buy a cock ring for his ex? Dan explained that she was dating a much older man who was having trouble sustaining erections.

When I've recounted this story to friends over the years, most people cannot believe a woman would ask her ex-boyfriend to buy a sex aid. These friends don't know Dan, who's so forthright and unpretentious that these things that might otherwise make some guys uncomfortable are non-issues with him. This was a pre-Viagra, pre-Internet era. The former girlfriend lived in a small town and didn't have access to a sex shop. Instead, she'd enlisted Dan's assistance in rescuing her sex life.

Dan planned to shop in the Combat Zone, which still thrived in Boston back then. It was an area of the city near downtown noteworthy for venues offering nude dancers, porn theaters, and sex shops. It also abounded with sex workers. I decided to join him just to avoid sitting alone stewing for the rest of the evening. I didn't care what we did or how strange it was. As I waited for Dan to arrive, I changed my clothes, dressing completely in black as if embarking on a reconnaissance mission for the French Resistance.

Dan picked me up in his Jeep, and we headed off. Once we reached the sex shop, we both wandered around for a bit. The place was well lit, and no one inside gave me the creeps although some of the products did. They seemed invasive and painful, but that may have been the point. After a while, Dan bounced up to the sales counter and in his most cheerful and booming voice asked the clerk to see the store's selection of cock rings. Next, in an equally loud and cheerful voice, he requested that I join him at the counter, to solicit my opinion. He wanted to know which of the devices I thought he should buy.

I tried to apply common sense to the challenge. There were only two styles available. The first model featured black leather with silver snaps. I vetoed it, saying the leather and hardware might be intimidating for an older person. The second model, a plain rubber ring, came in sizes small, medium, and large. I instructed Dan not to purchase anything marked "small." The humiliating size would prevent any man from achieving an erection; sustaining one would be a pipe dream. Dan saw the wisdom of my assessment.

Dan then asked if he should buy the large or the medium ring. He quizzed me at full volume about my personal experience with the two sizes. I allowed that the large was within the realm of possibility, but the medium seemed more standard issue. I'm certain everyone in the store could hear his end of the conversation. Dissatisfied with my input, he continued to bombard me, as well as the clerk, with more questions.

Meanwhile, men walked into the store no doubt expecting to buy some stimulating device or literature with a reasonable amount of discretion but instead were confronted with an earsplitting discussion on the merits of different-sized cock rings.

This piece of impromptu theater went on for so long and so loudly, eventually the clerk offered Dan a three-for-the-price-of-two deal just to get rid of him. We left the store with all three rubber rings in a plain brown paper bag.

By the time Dan and I parted company for the night, I had been almost completely shaken out of my depression. To this day, I still don't know how much of our adventure was Dan amusing himself and how much was a deliberate attempt to pull me out of my blues.

My most recent fringe encounter with the sexually exotic involved bondage cuffs, a gift at my wedding shower. Some wedding showers have gift themes, like kitchenware or lingerie. Mine was a themeless, low-key affair held in a friend's living room. While cheerfully opening my gifts toward the end of a lovely afternoon, I came across a completely pedestrian-looking box. I unwrapped it and found black-and-purple leather bondage cuffs inside. Astonished, I could only laugh. To my relief, the elderly friend on the couch next to me chuckled. The couple who'd given me the cuffs informed our hostess that they'd had them custom made for me in my favorite color, purple. Unsure of what to do with them, I schlepped the cuffs home along with the rest of my gifts.

Once home, I showed them to Harry, my fiancé, and asked him, "Are we ever going to use these?" When he answered no, I decided to get rid of them, custom-made-with-love or not. But Harry urged me to keep them. Initially, I failed to understand his reasoning. Why keep them if we weren't going to use them? Harry replied that they were "too new" to give away. I knew what he was driving at. They were like bondage art, beautifully crafted and bizarrely pleasing to the eye. I placed them on a high shelf in the coat closet.

A year later, I concluded it was time to get rid of them. Their newness had lost its appeal. At the time, I worked for a large AIDS service agency, which organized Boston's annual AIDS Walk. The agency's philosophy was that in order to talk about AIDS, staff needed to be able to talk about sex, and in order to talk about sex, we had to work in a "sex friendly" environment. The office was filled with calendars of buff men and shapely women, all nude, in Pilates-like poses. The only compromise for sex-sensitive colleagues: post-its covering the models' genitalia.

The agency conducted internal and external fund raising each year for the Walk. The month before the event, a multitude of goods and services were sold or auctioned off via internal e-mail, the proceeds going to the fundraising effort. Selling my custom-made bondage cuffs by silent auction on e-mail seemed the perfect way to dispose of them. I received a half-dozen inquiries, and they eventually sold for thirty-five dollars.

Many of my colleagues were eager to know who purchased the cuffs, but I promised to keep the buyer confidential. I've never disclosed her identity. The cuffs elevated me from the level of average, married, straight girl to instant member of the cool club among my freewheeling and lively colleagues. They must have forgotten that the cuffs were an unused gift I off-loaded for charity, which I'd explained in my sales pitch.

I must admit that, at best, I've only brushed against the edges of the sexually exotic: tempting a boyfriend with a fantasy never to be fulfilled, assisting in the purchase of a sex aid for a stranger, and receiving a sex toy I never used. But if my intimate life has lacked certain exotic qualities, I don't have complaints about it. Not feeling too choosy these days, I'd be happy to simply *have* a love life again. I'd be satisfied with something moderately sweet, like the ending of every movie based on a Nicholas Sparks novel.

I hope the participants at the next Tantra Puja gathering have a good time dancing semi-nude in the semi-dark. I'd like to imagine that the Crypt did a brisk business liquidating their overstock of handcuffs and brought an added bit of pleasure into its customers' lives. After all, if I'm not going to have any fun in that special way, I'd like to believe someone else, somewhere, is.

Chapter 10, 2005g

THE REAL THING

Sometimes it's best to give the search for romantic love a rest and focus on more immediate and accessible forms of affection. For example, the love of a good cat.

With a cat, there are primarily two kinds of love. The first is expressed when a need must be met. My cat, Zoe, rubs against me, gives me delicate little kitty kisses, and then looks soulfully into my eyes. This is the love that says, "Feed me now." Once food is placed before her, the loving ceases. The second, more intense love, which comes from a deep feline instinct, occurs when she senses I'm ill and licks my face with her little raspy tongue. The grooming/loving usually leaves me with a sore face and covered in kitty spit. If I'm resting during this display of affection, I have to rouse myself to wash my face. This kind of love feels heartfelt, but not particularly helpful.

When hard pressed, I'll admit to a third type of love, one that has impelled Zoe to sleep by my shoulder for the last sixteen years. This love also drives her to sit on my chest, nose to nose, sometimes with a paw resting on my cheek as I watch television in bed—the real thing. It's why I subject myself to feeding her disgusting wet cat food and scooping poop.

I hate it when people refer to their pets as their children. Do these folks have children? Here's a test: If there's a fire, whom do you rescue first? I'll bet it's not the cat. A vast difference exists between creatures on all fours and two-legged humans with opposable thumbs. If Zoe had them, I'd make her open the cans of revolting cat food herself. She could scoop her own poop, and I'd be much happier.

Although a pet is not a child, I believe Zoe has English skills that she withholds from me. Her vocabulary is limited, but when I encourage her to jump on the bed after a failed attempt, she does, and if I announce that she's about to be fed (no hand signals or other types of movement on my part to indicate my intention), she immediately gets the drift.

My attachment to Zoe is deep, and I'm ridiculously besotted with her. When she goes to God, I plan to sit Shiva for a week as Jewish law dictates. Loved ones can come to my house, bring me food, and help me mourn. Unfortunately, I'm fairly certain that my employer, the County of San Diego, doesn't include geriatric cats on their list of loved ones meriting bereavement leave. I'll have to rend my clothes while serving the county's needs when she dies. Let them think I'm a slob. I won't care; I'll be in mourning.

My mother gave me a cat at the beginning of second grade, for which I had full responsibility. Sometimes these responsibilities were completely inappropriate. At ten years old, I stood alone on a New York City street corner, holding my cat, trying to hail a cab. Mom had instructed me to wrap my sick pet in a towel and take her to the vet.

This was not the way to transport a cat and definitely not the way to treat an over-bred, high-strung Siamese. As a teenager in California, shortly after I received my driver's license, Mom again directed me to take one of the cats to the vet. She'd failed to purchase a cat carrier, so I tied the cat to the seat of the car with the dog's leash. This was also not the correct way to transport a cat. But I loved the cats, so I tried to take care of them in what was obviously not a fully functional household.

By the time I was twenty-nine years old, I'd lived without a pet for ten years and missed having one keenly. I'd just moved into an apartment building that allowed cats, and I was thrilled. I planned to adopt a male kitten in the hopes it would grow into a big, dopey tomcat, like the one my father and stepmother had when I was growing up.

I called the pound regularly to check on the availability of male kittens. Weeks went by until they finally had a litter with males. My friend Roberta and I drove to the pound, intent on taking one of the boy kittens home. Roberta came along to drive so I could bond with my new baby as it sat in my lap *in its carrier.*

When we arrived at the pound, we saw two rows of cages, upper and lower, on our left. Roberta sprinted down the row, surveying all the cats, but I decided to meander my way over to the boy kittens. Facing the upper row of cages, I spotted a sweet little gray-and-white cat that appeared to be about six to nine months old. She looked at me with hope in her eyes, but I passed her by in my search for a boy kitten. I looked into the second cage and saw another cat who seemed about the same age, a little black-and-blond tabby. I meant to continue on my way to the younger kittens, but the little tabby yowled at me. I'm not hardhearted so I paused to coo at her. When she didn't stop yowling, I opened her cage, took her out, and held her on my chest. This was a monumental error. The cat began to purr and nuzzle. I told her, "Look, I'm here for a boy kitten, not a girl. Not you." She looked into my eyes, rubbed her little face against mine, and I fell in love. I would have had to be semi-vegetative to resist. Instead, I succumbed and told her, "Well, okay, you're not what I want, but I guess you're coming home with me." Roberta beckoned me over to look at the other cats, but I never made it past the second cage.

Instead of adopting a male kitten, which I fantasized would grow to be big and dumb, I returned home with a smart, almost fully grown, female midget. At her heaviest, she weighed about eight-and-a-half pounds. Not at all what I'd thought I wanted.

But like all true love, you give in to greater forces than yourself. I always tell Zoe she's smarter than me although I believe she already knows this. She chose me against my will, using forceful seduction.

These days, I almost exclusively refer to her as "my needy geriatric cat." I know we're cruising on borrowed time. For the last few years, I've felt as if I'm married to a seventy-five-year-old. We could have many more years of bliss together, or she could go at any time. She nearly died last winter but pulled through so now our time together is more precious than ever.

In movies, sometimes male characters successfully woo their female partners against the women's better judgment and efforts to resist. The example that immediately springs to mind is a great German movie from a few years back, *Mostly Martha*, in which, as part of the subplot, a highly neurotic chef is won over by another chef who works in her kitchen even though she initially resents and avoids him. I have one friend with a story like this, and it's touching. But this sort of thing never happens to most women. No smart man has chosen me and then wooed me until I saw the wisdom of his actions. I suppose the love of a good cat, who picked me out against my better judgment, will have to suffice. It's been a good deal.

Chapter 11, 2005h

TOO MUCH INFORMATION

I like to think of myself as a nice person, a trait that's part of my self-concept as a social worker, but I don't want to hear about erectile dysfunction when I'm eating dinner. Not a little bit, not ever.

This is my fault. I usually eat dinner while watching the evening news. Almost every guide to healthful eating instructs against this. I'm sorry, but single, middle-aged women didn't write those guides. If cooking for one ranks high among the world's most boring activities, then eating solo follows right after. I need some diversion while I eat, and television works well. Recently, however, I've found myself overwhelmed during dinner by ads for erectile dysfunction medications. This isn't what I want to see as I try to enjoy my vegetarian lasagna. Cialis and Levitra, the long-lasting medications, have become the bane of my dinner hour.

The evening news is challenging lately in general. Unless it's the kind of day when Deep Throat outs himself, I can count on the death toll from our dual wars in Iraq and Afghanistan being the lead national story every night. I try to stay in the kitchen for the first few minutes of each broadcast. I can hear the news from there but miss the gory visuals. In addition to war, I can now, with a fair degree of certainty, also rely on seeing at least one ad for Cialis and/or Levitra per meal. It's a major drag.

Part of the problem is my imagination, which is what the advertisers are counting on; minds like mine create their own mental images, images banned on primetime television. For example, one of the ads depicts two people sitting side by side in outdoor bathtubs holding hands. The tubs are big, old-fashioned types, which enhances the romance. They're situated on a hillcrest and face a scenic view. I know the point of these medications is to be long lasting, but my mind stays focused on the immediate situation. I wonder if one member of the hand-holding couple will jump out of his tub and into hers, and then the two of them will go at it like drunken kids at a frat party in *Animal House.* Or do they contain their libidos until they hustle to an indoor locale? I'd like to know.

Another mini-scene in these ads shows two people in sexual precontemplation in what looks like a bookstore. They're sidling up to each other and lightly touching one another in order to signal their readiness for fornication. I understand the implications. If this were real life and not a nano-scene in a television ad, everyone in the bookstore would understand it, too. Every time I see this ad, I'm reminded of my friend, Robert. In his twenties, he enjoyed an affair with a married librarian. Robert told me they often snuck off together and had sex in the library stairwell. Robert liked adrenaline rushes, so I understood the appeal for him. I always wondered if some hapless person, committed to exercise, ever ran into them fulfilling their needs in the stairwell between the classics and science floors.

When I see the ad with the nuzzling couple in the bookstore, I question what happened post nuzzle. Did they leap into their car and speed off, as if one of them were going into sugar shock and needed a quick fix from Dairy Queen? Or did they handle their lust the way Robert did and head for the nearest stairwell, taking care of matters there? My lesson from this: a vivid imagination isn't always a good thing.

In another ad, a woman curls up in a chair in a seductive pose, saying, "My man takes Levitra" and referring to its "strong, long-lasting effect." Dear Lord in Heaven, how am I supposed to enjoy my Ben and Jerry's listening to stuff like that?

This is just so wrong, juxtaposed with the evening news. It's jarring. I don't want to think about "long-lasting effects" twenty seconds after listening to the President's plan to change social security. It's too big a mental leap to make at the end of the workday. I can barely handle the social security matter as a stand-alone issue.

I'm not a prude or against sex on screen. Although I don't like porn, I'm actually pro-sex on the big screen. I like all sex in good movies: heterosexual and same-sex romps. But not with dinner, and not after a day of social work or after listening to a news segment about nuclear proliferation.

I'm not insensitive to people with erectile dysfunction. I care about the non-erect. If my happy parts no longer worked as desired, I'd be deeply upset. Even though they are decommissioned right now, I like knowing they're in good working order. It's comforting to know that, like the Army Reserves, they are prepared to serve when called to duty.

I'm not completely unfamiliar with this issue. I first made its acquaintance during with my brief fling with Eli when I was twenty-three. I met him when I called my friend, Kim, in Seattle, after I moved, to give her my new contact information. Kim lived in shared housing with Eli and several other people. He answered the phone (a landline, since no one had cell phones yet) and seemed thrilled to speak to me. Eli explained that Kim talked about me often. One thing led to another, and by the call's end, we'd agreed to mail each other our photos and speak again soon. After three weeks of phone calls, he flew down to my place in the Bay Area to spend a long weekend with me.

I picked Eli up at the San Francisco airport early in the evening. We had a quick dinner at a completely unmemorable restaurant and then headed home. Eli and I were so relaxed with each other that I can't completely recall how we ended up in bed. I believe it went something like this: I said, "I'm tired. Let's go to bed." So, we did. Together.

I know—this sounds so slutty now. But in the early1980s, every well-adjusted woman my age who I knew and who wasn't in a long-term relationship and whose religious convictions didn't prohibit premarital sex behaved exactly the way I did. Back then, we stressed about relationships. We didn't stress as much about sex and instead simply enjoyed ourselves. My friends and I hadn't begun to worry about AIDS yet, and wisely or not, we just took our chances on catching other sexually transmitted diseases. First date, second date, third date—whichever, my friends and I fell into bed with whomever we wanted to and without much fanfare.

During the first night of Eli's visit, sex happened. Sex happened again the next morning. We spent our first day together, walking and picnicking on the beach at Half Moon Bay. Affectionate and playful together, we laughed and held hands. The second night, sex began to happen, and then Eli's plumbing failed him, and sex stopped happening. The same thing occurred the next morning. I didn't mind. I'd enjoyed his visit up to that point, and I didn't need to have sex twice a day every day.

On the second day of his visit, Eli began to withdraw his affection. By evening, he was grouchy, and there were no more attempts at sex. He was so unpleasant by the third day that I loaned him my car so he could take care of some business in Oakland—just to get rid of him. I drove a car owned by my mother, and I'd promised her I wouldn't lend it to anyone. I felt bad about breaking my word, but I didn't want to spend another day with Eli, who continued to sulk.

After Eli flew home to Seattle, I was chatting with a friend and mentioned to her his sudden aloofness and sullen behavior. This friend was a good twenty years older than I. I was so young and naïve that she needed to connect the dots for me. It honestly hadn't occurred to me that Eli's sudden change in demeanor might be connected to his penis problem. My friend practically shouted, "That's not normal for a twenty-eight-year-old!" It wasn't whether I thought his erectile dysfunction was normal. It was a non-issue for me and, so I'd assumed, a non-issue for him, too. I'd attributed his sullen behavior to a mystery element. God, was I stupid!

Of course, the poor guy had been mortified and embarrassed. Until I let him borrow my mother's car, he had no way to escape except into himself. He certainly could have used some "long-lasting effects." A few pills might have seen him through the entire three-day weekend without a worry, easy as pie.

Nevertheless, Eli shouldn't be entirely let off the hook. While Mom's car was in his possession, he received a parking ticket, which he failed to pay. As the owner, Mom received the overdue notice for the ticket, thus learning I'd let someone borrow her car. Mom was remarkably good natured about my betraying her trust. I made three pointed phone calls to Eli before he paid the forty dollars he owed me for the ticket. Afterward, I felt much less sympathetic about his unfortunate penis problem.

There are women for whom a working penis isn't critical to sexual satisfaction. I remember watching an Oprah show during the late eighties or early nineties that addressed this issue. The show featured a woman who'd married her paraplegic husband straight out of high school. She explained that no one could understand why she wed him, given his level of disability. At a critical juncture in the show, Oprah asked her directly if they were able to have sex. With a big smile and a no-nonsense attitude, she replied, "Everything but intercourse." Oprah didn't push the matter further.

There's also something to be said for creativity. I understand that most of us like access to the full sexual menu rather than a meal made up only of appetizers. But the truth is, if you're a woman, you can have the appetizers and go directly from there to dessert without going anywhere near the entrées. It happens all the time.

There are some good examples of this in movie-land. Am I the only one who remembers the rocking hot sex scene from *Coming Home*, the 1978 movie starring Jane Fonda and Jon Voight? In the film, Jon portrayed a paraplegic Vietnam veteran. Jane had the most realistic sex I'd ever seen on screen. Mom said she could have sworn Jane actually had an orgasm. I hadn't needed to hear this commentary from my mother, but I couldn't argue her point. Both Jane and Jon won academy awards for their performances in the film.

Reflecting on the Levitra ad, I believed it should feature a man instead of a woman. A man could talk about his need to be erect and functional—this is a man's issue. As long as men are willing to fulfill women's needs creatively, they can manage quite well.

The last time I spoke to Robert, he told me he'd begun to take Cialis. He wanted to know if I'd heard of it. I ranted a little at first about all the ads I'd seen on TV, but then answered yes, I had. Despite my aversion to the Cialis ad, I'm happy for Robert. He's been taking antidepressants for years. The drugs decreased his libido, a painful reality for him and his wife. Robert says Cialis is working. Maybe instead of these annoying ads, Robert and his spouse could submit a personal, videotaped testimonial about the healing effects the medication had on their marriage. Then I wouldn't be so annoyed. Instead, I'd be glad to know someone's life was back on track, and maybe I could enjoy my dinner again.

ON THE OTHER HAND

It's been a long time since I needed to ask someone to remove their hands from my nether regions. This sort of thing happened to me in my twenties and early thirties, but I hadn't been forced to fend someone off in this particular manner for over a dozen years.

Darius and I were on my couch engaging in activities typical of second dates. Suddenly, I felt his hand inside my favorite body cavity. Whoa! What in the name of all that is holy was that? I asked him to "not do that" and then forcibly removed his hand. Looking Darius in the eye I stated, "Let's keep things above the equator." In retrospect, it wasn't the best moment to employ a metaphor because within a minute his hand roamed back to where it had just been. I grabbed his wrist, pulled his hand out of my undergarments, and firmly stated, "I'm not ready to have sex with you."

His reply? "That's not sex."

Several thoughts went through my mind. The first: "You must belong to the Bill Clinton School of Sex." The second: "When any part of *your body* is in that part of *my body*, we're having sex." What I actually said was, "If your hand is in my ___ (I used a vulgar term to catch his attention), that's sex." This scenario may sound like a distressing violation. It wasn't, but it *was* a big surprise.

In the past, during similar encounters, I'd always worn blue jeans—the dating equivalent of barbed wire on the beaches at Normandy. The barriers weren't insurmountable, but they required excessive will and skill to traverse. Usually when a man wanted to get into my pants, he'd work from north to south. I could always stop him at the Mason-Dixon line (my waist) whenever I wanted to. Not expecting to be groped in this manner, I'd dressed in a skirt for the July weather, not for a horny man with no dating manners.

Although I've engaged more than once in spontaneous sex early in relationships, I choose to participate on a case-by-case basis, the operative word being *choose*. With only a short warm-up, Darius could have enjoyed the entire enchilada, but he was both impatient and foolish.

How did I get myself into this situation? How indeed. Darius's e-mail to me had popped up out of nowhere in July. I assumed I'd answered his personal ad weeks or months ago because he appeared with no forewarning.

We exchanged e-mails for a few days and then agreed to meet. Darius wanted to go to a movie, so we arranged to see the early afternoon show of *War of the Worlds* on the fourth of July. Our first date was a comedy of errors. I sat in the lobby of the movie theater, where we'd planned to rendezvous, but Darius never arrived. At showtime, I went into the theater and looked for any guy who might be sitting on an aisle, craning his neck when someone walked by. Everyone seemed to be intently watching the previews, not watching for a stray woman stumbling around in the dark.

I walked back to the lobby. At the time I rarely left my cell phone on and didn't give out the number. When I turned on my phone to call Darius, I noticed a message. Darius didn't know about my cell phone issues. When I'd asked him to call me on my home phone if he needed to change our plans, the information hadn't computed, and he'd pressed the return feature on his cell phone to call me at 10:00 a.m. that day.

His message stated he needed to delay our date until that night or the next one because he needed to do laundry. This was the most pathetic excuse for canceling a date I'd ever heard. When I'd spoken to Darius two nights before, he explained that he'd recently moved into an apartment complex without a laundry room and had accumulated a month's worth of dirty clothes. I should have taken this as a clue about his life management skills, but I know men are often different from women about certain domestic tasks so didn't dwell on the matter. When I listened to his message, I couldn't believe that a day-and-a-half later he still hadn't gotten his laundry washed and canceled our date on a *national holiday* in order to do the job.

I called Darius and told him his excuse was completely lame. With nothing to lose, I gave him the hard time he deserved. When Darius realized I was waiting for him at the movie theater, he tried to redeem himself. He offered to come over immediately and watch the movie. I explained that it had already started, so he volunteered to drive to the mall to grab a bite to eat with me.

We sat at an outdoor café and engaged in all the usual first date small talk. Darius seemed sincerely interested in getting acquainted and was a sweet goofball. We enjoyed our hour together, and he promised to call. All was forgiven.

I heard from him a couple of days later. Darius wanted to see me again but struggled, trying to decide where and when to meet. Although he was thirty-five years old, he didn't seem to grasp the basics of asking out women. I found this surprising for someone who held a master's degree in public health, but this deficit wasn't high enough on my list of dating sins to forego a second rendezvous. We made arrangements for a walk after work on Friday. He won points when he called Friday evening to say he'd be a bit late.

Prior to the groping, we took a quiet, hour-long stroll and then hung out on my couch, talking, watching television, looking at some of my twenty-plus photo albums, and enjoying some nooky-free cuddling.

As ten o'clock approached, Darius announced that he needed to get going. I figured things had progressed romantically as far as they were going to for the evening. But when he hugged me goodbye, his hands began roaming, and he clearly became aroused.

I invited him to return to the couch but added that he couldn't spend the night. Matters progressed with startling speed. As his hand invaded my crotch, he seemed completely absorbed in his own arousal. I might as well have been a blow-up doll.

Shortly after I removed his hand from my underpants for the second time, Darius took a deep breath and muttered something about needing to go home; otherwise, he "would have to spend the night." I thought him presumptuous to assume he'd be sleeping with me, but I decided to let it go since he was heading out the door. Darius gave me a long bear hug goodbye, but he appeared lost in his own thoughts and feelings.

We planned a third date for a few nights later. When I got home from work on date night, I found a message from Darius saying he couldn't make it and would have to take a rain check. I'm not adept at speaking foreign languages. At the end of eighth grade, I received straight As except for one D—in Spanish. I had a Spanish tutor and worked hard for my D. But I pride myself in my increasing ability to understand man-speak. "I can't make it and will have to take a rain check" translates to "Because you wouldn't let me feel you up on the second date, I've decided there won't be a third date." Already ambivalent about the third date, I didn't care if I never saw Darius again.

I spoke to my Uncle Jon the night of the canceled date and told him about my two dates with Darius. Everyone who knows Jon loves him. He's completely accepting and nonjudgmental but doesn't hesitate to give pointed avuncular advice. Jon summarized this particular dating episode by stating, "He's not the right guy for you." Never were truer words spoken.

On the other hand, how great is it that an attractive thirty-five year-old lusted after me? He wasn't the right man for me, but I didn't care. Instead, I felt comforted and encouraged knowing I still have it going on at the mature age of forty-five. What a delightful mid-life surprise!

Since my date with Darius, I've decided to adopt a one-strike-and-you're-out policy. When Darius canceled our date on the fourth of July for something as mundane as laundry, I'd have been wise to cut him loose. If a man can't put his best foot forward at the beginning of a relationship when he should be trying to make a good impression, he probably never will. The state of California may have a three-strikes law, but I've decided to be less generous. From now on, one strike with me, and you're toast.

During our second date, Darius had mentioned that *Swingers* was one of his favorite movies. I love this movie, too. It features two buddies and their circle of friends. One of the men, Jon Favreau, is emotionally paralyzed after a breakup with his girlfriend and can't stop obsessing about her. He wallows in his depression despite the best efforts of his buddy to cajole him out of it and get him laid. It's a sweet movie with sharp writing. You'd think that someone with such good taste in movies, particularly a movie about dating and relationships, would have handled himself better. I've been meaning to rent *Swingers* to see how it's held up over the years. Because, while men will come and go, I can always depend on a good movie.

Chapter 13, 2005j

NEXT!

I've been crying for a week because Saul didn't ask me for a second date. This over-the-top reaction is a complete surprise. I'm incredulous at my weepiness. It's as though I've been overcome by the ghost of my adolescence and want my adulthood back.

If there's any doubt that we don't control all the events of our lives, dating serves as a useful reminder. This is especially true for women, who traditionally haven't assumed the role of initiator. I don't care what anyone says—the fundamental rules of dating haven't changed much since my grandmothers were doing it. Although it's now socially acceptable for women to initiate relationships, most of the time men still do it, and men still seem to be in the driver's seat when it comes to asking for second and third dates. While the earth won't spin off its axis if women initiate second dates, I believe it's wiser to wait for men to make the move. As most women know, men can barely handle the basics of dating using the *old* rules. If we start changing them, they'll have no idea what to do. In addition, I prefer knowing that a man wants to see me again. The only way to find that out is to wait.

But waiting is torture. It hasn't gotten any better in the last twenty-five years. The only improvement over the last quarter century is the use of answering machines, texts, and e-mails. Never again does anyone need to sit around waiting for the phone to ring. Aside from advancements in technology, though, it might as well be the 1970s.

At the moment, it seems as if I've time-traveled back to the eighties. I'm feeling as vulnerable as I ever did in my youth despite myriad dating experiences and adventures.

Here's how I happen to be reliving the worst parts of my distant romantic past: A couple of weeks ago, my colleague Yaffa set me up with Saul, who attends her synagogue. I've recently begun occasionally attending synagogue although Yaffa is an observant orthodox Jew and I'm a mostly non-observant reform one. I love the warmth of Yaffa's congregation and her scholarly, funny rabbi. I decided if I'm going to learn about my religion, I might as well learn about it from people who are deeply committed to practicing the rituals of our shared ancestors.

Dating is serious business for the orthodox. Its primary purpose is to find a spouse. This led many of my friends to ask me if I'd consider marrying an orthodox Jew. I replied, "Sure. I'm trying to be more observant, and with a loving spouse to support me, I'd gladly do my best to be orthodox." And even within orthodoxy, there's a continuum of observance. Not all orthodox communities are restrictive and conservative, like the one depicted in the film, *A Price Above Rubies*, in which Renée Zellweger feels oppressed and controlled by her religion. Many orthodox Jews fit seamlessly into mainstream American culture, like Sam, the baseball loving "pickle man" in the movie *Crossing Delancey*. So, when Yaffa offered to set me up with someone from her synagogue, I happily accepted.

Most people hate blind dates, but I enjoy them. I like getting to know someone new, even briefly. I relish the challenge of making conversation with a stranger. Last summer, my family purposely placed me next to an incredibly boring man at a dinner party. I found myself saying things like, "And what *is it* about golf that you enjoy?" I managed to keep the conversation going through the dessert course, and I didn't mind at all. Occasionally, I've had blind dates with men who are so inept I've wanted to flee after ten minutes, but that only happens about once a decade.

Yaffa gave Saul my contact information in the middle of the week, and he called me the following Monday. He was soft spoken and not particularly chatty on the phone. After fifteen minutes of conversation, I realized Saul was simply shy. But he stayed on the phone with me for over an hour until we both needed to wind down our evenings.

Our date started out slow, but I quickly got used to the rhythm of his pauses, and by mid-evening, I learned to rest a little during the conversation because he inevitably rallied. I discovered Saul was funny, and he made the date easy. He picked me up at my apartment, made choosing a restaurant a no-fuss decision, and opened the car door for me. He also picked up the check so fast I didn't have an opportunity to ask if I could contribute.

A bright man, Saul had a PhD in astral physics and worked on a computerized surveillance program for the military. We talked about our families, synagogue, and nothing in particular.

Before the date, I had asked Yaffa about inviting Saul up for coffee, assuming I liked him sufficiently to extend our time together after dinner. I wanted to be sure that he'd understand coffee really meant coffee, rather than a veiled offer to indulge in any non-orthodox activity on the first date. Yaffa assured me Saul would take an invitation for coffee at face value.

When Saul drove to my building after dinner, I asked him up and was pleased when he agreed. As the evening progressed, I liked Saul more and more. He was easy to talk to and just the slightest bit flirty.

We were happily chatting when Saul suddenly announced that he needed to leave; the cat was "getting" to him. Huh? The cat was what? It turned out he's allergic to cats. To *my* cat. To my baby, Zoe. He said meeting me had been "great" and dinner was "lovely." Then, he hightailed it out of my apartment with a speed that left me confused and crestfallen.

Our date was on a Wednesday, and when I hadn't heard from him by late Sunday night, I began to cry. I'd been watching a DVD of *The Sopranos*. There's enough human drama in each episode to make anyone weep. Monday night I viewed another *Sopranos* episode and found myself crying again. I started to wonder what was wrong with me—seriously. Two nights later, I continued to cry, but not as much or for as long.

I would find myself peacefully watching *The Sopranos*, which should have been completely distracting, and the next thing I knew, tears rolled down my cheeks, prompting me to hit the pause button.

What was wrong with me? Startled and disappointed when Saul bolted out of my apartment, I figured that I probably wouldn't see him again. Yaffa, however, had a different spin on it. She thought Saul had petered out that night, but she didn't believe it was a predictor of his future intentions. She didn't think the cat allergy was a deal-breaker, either. Saul was looking for a Jewish woman who would honor his religious practices and share his beliefs. There weren't many of us around San Diego. Yaffa thought if he were interested enough, he'd take allergy shots.

We never know why someone doesn't call back. My friend Gabe ran a personal ad in a Boston newspaper for two years in the nineties. Women continually rejected him until he met his wife, to whom he's been happily married for ten years. But during the two years of endless blind dates, he'd complain that women didn't give him a chance. I repeatedly told him that the women didn't know him well enough to reject him on a personal level. He just wasn't the type they were looking for.

I'm not so far gone that I'm unable to apply this same logic to myself. I don't feel personally rejected. I know Saul had his reasons for not asking for a second date. Maybe it involved the cat, or maybe I might not have been what Saul wanted.

But as I'd sat across from him at the dining table that once belonged to my grandmother, I'd thought, "You're exactly what I want." Until the end of our date, I believed he'd been enjoying himself as much as I was. Now I know that my initial response to Saul's sudden departure was probably correct. I'll never know why, and it doesn't matter.

Usually, I can predict if someone is going to ask me out, but there have been exceptions. Ezra, whom I dated in the summer of 1984, took a couple of weeks to call after he met me at a singles dance. After a week, I was certain I'd never hear from him. Whatever delayed him wasn't a lack of interest; I'd had to pry him off for most of our first date.

Most notably was the delay in hearing from Alan. I met him on an early morning flight from San Francisco to New York when I was twenty-eight. I'd planned to catch up on sleep during the flight. Alan sat three seats away in a four-seat row. We began chatting over the two empty seats between us as we settled in for the flight. After two hours of talking, he moved into the seat next to me. By the third hour of the flight, I realized I wasn't going to get any sleep, and by the end of the flight I'd invited Alan to visit me in Boston where I lived.

A doctor from Australia, Alan had been on his way to England where he planned to take the British medical boards. He said he'd be back in New York in two weeks and would call me then. Crushed when I didn't hear from him, I couldn't believe my perceptions were so off. But at the beginning of February, he called. A snafu with his boards had delayed him in London for a couple of weeks. He visited Boston in the middle of February for three of the most enchanting days I've ever experienced. (Afterward, he flew home to Australia—too far away for a long-distance relationship in a pre-e-mail, pre-Skype era.)

I don't know whether I'll hear from Saul again. We never know. But it's time to stop crying, pull myself together, and move on. My friends Laverne and Babs yell, "Next!" every time I tell them some potential romance hasn't panned out. (This was a good decade and a half before the top-forty hit by Ariana Grande, "Thank U, Next.") Laverne and Babs are caring, but their view of my love life is pragmatic. They don't want me to sit around and feel sorry for myself. They always urge me to move forward, to find true love. So *next* it is.

Joanna J. Charnas

Chapter 14, 2005k

WHAT WOULD MOM SAY NOW?

Mom died tragically at forty-nine, in large part because of unrestrained excesses and intractable willfulness. She had untreated Bipolar Disorder but was also brilliant, funny, and possessed a powerful, Brando-like charisma. When she died, many of her friends told me she'd been the brightest woman they'd ever known. When Mom's perceptions weren't clouded by the skewed vision of her imbalanced chemistry or controlled by her abundant insecurities, she could be deeply insightful and articulate.

Mom passed away almost twenty years ago, but she continues to be a strong influence on my life. I find myself wondering what she'd say about recent events with Saul. When I told Yaffa I hadn't heard from Saul for over a week after our first date, she offered to call him to find out how he felt about our evening together. This is a standard practice in Orthodox Judaism—intermediaries are often utilized to manage the first few dates of a relationship. As Yaffa explained, the use of intermediaries reduces much of the anxiety either person might feel regarding the courtship process. I could have used Orthodoxy in my twenties—I'd never have wasted endless hours wondering if the phone would ring. Grateful for Yaffa's help, I happily accepted her offer.

When Yaffa spoke to Saul, he reported that he'd had a good time on our date. I didn't press her for details, and I'm not sure she had any to give. Saul told Yaffa he was thinking about what to do next. After my four-day crying jag, I found this news oddly comforting. I liked knowing that he took dating me seriously and treated a potential relationship with gravity.

A few days after Saul talked to Yaffa, he called to ask me out. On our second date, we took a long walk followed by kosher sorbet at my apartment. Saul still seemed painfully shy, but this didn't bother me. I knew he'd need time to relax in my company. We had our third date a week and a half later. It started at 9:00 p.m. on Saturday night, when Shabbos was over. I thought this was hysterically funny. I'd never begun a date so late unless I was already sleeping with someone. Saul and I attended a 9:50 showing of *Asylum*, a movie in which Natasha Richardson has an illicit affair with a mental patient at the psychiatric hospital where her husband works. After the movie, Saul joked that he'd enjoyed the scene in which Natasha's character reposes, naked, in a bathtub. I thought, "Good, he's relaxing," and I felt optimistic about seeing him again.

Then, I didn't hear from him. "Okay," I thought. "That's that." The intense melancholy that overtook me after our first date and Saul's subsequent silence had mercifully departed, and I returned to normal dating mode. Sometimes, men just don't call. After only three dates, Saul didn't owe me an explanation.

Two weeks after that last date, Saul surprised me following Saturday religious services by going out of his way to talk to me. He'd previously told me he didn't usually stick around for Kiddush, the Jewish equivalent of coffee and cookies except with much more food. (We are Jewish, after all.) Saul clearly waited to approach me when I was alone. We spent fifteen minutes together, catching up on the previous two weeks of our lives. I enjoyed chatting with him but wondered why he had gone out of his way to talk to me. I was confused when we said goodbye, and I still am.

As I've thought about Saul over the last few days, I've also been thinking about all of the relationship advice Mom gave me in my twenties, before she died. I wonder what advice she'd give me now. I'm sure she would say I'm entitled to be with someone who isn't conflicted or confused about me, that I should date someone who's less reserved and more enthusiastic. Mom would point out that I've spent too much time trying to figure out what's going on and not enough time feeling good.

My mother always wanted the best for me and seemed mostly unaware that she didn't provide it herself. Her fundamental inability to meet her own needs consumed her. She didn't have the internal resources to give my brother and me the basic parenting we needed. My childhood was so distressing, it's reminiscent of *Mommie Dearest*, the movie based on the book by Christina Crawford about her childhood with *her* mother,

Joan Crawford. The movie has become a cult classic based on the over-the-top, campy performance of Faye Dunaway. Mom loaned me her copy of the book when it was published in 1978 with the proviso that I never mention the similarities between her and Joan Crawford. I was surprised she had any insight into her bad behavior, something she never acknowledged again. There's no doubt that Mom loved us as much as her limitations allowed. So, now I believe Mom would say that Saul isn't good enough for me. She would tell me to spend my energies on someone who's excited and happy to be dating me.

Prone to manic, illogical, rages reflecting her own unhappy life, Mom sometimes had a loose grip on reality. Other times, she was dead on the money. As an adult, I didn't want to hear her advice about my love life. But she was twenty-two years older than me and could often tell when things weren't going well long before I could. I might have spared myself much of the pain or disappointment of my youthful love life if I'd listened to her. Because I'm still her child, I have avoided her as a spirit guide and gone my own way, just as I often did when she was alive.

Nevertheless, the ghost of my crazy, charismatic mother whispering in my ear is a powerful force. Maybe now, when I'm just four years younger than she was when she died, I'll be smarter than I was during her life. I'll pay attention to the advice I know she'd give me—to let Saul go entirely and not step backward into something that's been more confounding than rewarding. I'd like to believe Mom would tell me to hold out for someone who brings me joy, even when faced with the slim pickings of middle age.

That's what Mom would say. I'm certain of it, and this time I'll listen.

LATE BLOOMER

I've always been a late bloomer. I didn't learn how to read until four months before my seventh birthday and after I'd already flunked first grade. Clumsy and uncoordinated, I failed at most sports, right up until the moment, at thirty-two, when I broke three stacked wooden boards with my bare hand, completing the test for my black belt in Tae Kwon Do. So, discovering that I'm hot at this late stage of life doesn't completely surprise me. I don't mean Sharon Stone in *Basis Instinct* hot, or super-model-getting-older-but-still-looking-great hot. I'm more of the average-forty-five-year-old-aging-well kind of hot. But I've never felt this way before, so the change is a revelation.

The feeling finally gelled for me recently while attending a one-day seminar on Dialectical Behavioral Therapy (DBT). DBT is the treatment of choice for patients living with Borderline Personality Disorder. Signing in for the seminar, I ran into Rick. He's a licensed marriage family therapist, and I'm a licensed clinical social worker. Although neither of us earns our living as psychotherapists, our clinical licenses require that we obtain continuing education.

Rick and I first met at a Red Cross emergency center after the San Diego wildfires of 2003. Named the Cedar Fire, this blaze was actually fourteen separate fires that destroyed two thousand homes and scorched over 750,000 acres. It began in late October and wasn't completely extinguished until the middle of November. The County of San Diego employs Rick and me. After the fire, our branches of county government, Mental Health, and Aging and Independence Services, sent us to one of the emergency centers servicing fire victims. We'd both volunteered for a ten-hour shift.

During one of the lulls in the heartbreaking flow of fire victims, Rick and I began to chat. I learned he was an Italian American from New Jersey, lived with two cats, had recently broken up with his girlfriend, and planned to buy a condo. I also discovered that Rick loved movies, the same kind of films I enjoy, and went to them with a similar, obsessive regularity. At the end of our shift, Rick slipped me his cell phone number and suggested I call him so we could catch a movie together. I couldn't believe I got hit on doing my civic duty in the aftermath of a natural disaster.

We saw one film together, and then there was a single voice-mail message before the holidays assuring me that when he returned from visiting his elderly mother in New Jersey, we'd go out again. After New Year's we exchanged several e-mails, but then he disappeared, leaving me disappointed and a little annoyed.

Rick had emphasized his preference for matinees over evening shows. Based on these indications and several other telling details, I strongly suspected he might still be living with his girlfriend. After I recovered from my disappointment, I didn't think about him again.

I ran into Rick at another continuing education seminar about six months after our date. Rick noticed me during a break and initiated about five minutes of pleasant small talk. I remember thinking, "Oh, we're going to be adults about this." Since we'd behaved maturely the year before, I figured we'd be acting like grownups at the Dialectical Behavioral Therapy seminar. This is what I mean about being a late bloomer—I assumed there was reason and logic to interaction between the sexes. I should have known better.

Before the training began, I strolled over to the table where Rick parked himself to say hello. Instead of being receptive to my niceties, as he'd been the year before, he seemed intensely uncomfortable. I had no desire to torture him. So, I made my greetings brief, but I wondered what was going on.

My friend Yaffa, who also attended the seminar, had to clue me in. When she and I were heading toward the bathrooms during our first break, we found ourselves walking next to Rick. More small talk ensued. Rick still seemed jumpy, but he appeared less uncomfortable than he'd been a couple of hours earlier. We parted company outside the bathrooms.

Yaffa inquired about Rick later over lunch. I told her the story and questioned why he seemed as though he wanted to crawl out of his skin. Yaffa, who has laser-like perceptions, explained, "He's attracted to you, and he doesn't know what to do about it." Really? As soon as the words were out of her mouth, I knew Yaffa was right. I don't think of myself in those terms, or at least I didn't until that moment. I never believed I possessed the capacity to cause that kind of turmoil in a man.

In retrospect, my life began to change a couple years ago when I went on the Fifteen Pounds to Menopause Diet. I wanted to get down to a healthy weight before menopause when hormones might wreak havoc on my metabolism. The Fifteen Pounds to Menopause Diet, a weight loss plan of my own design, mostly involved deprivation. Over time, it turned into the Twenty-Five Pounds to Menopause Diet. After I lost the weight, many people questioned how I did it. I told anyone who asked that I'd been hungry for five months.

I'd been chubby intermittently since six years old, the year my parents separated. In first grade, I spent much of the time staring out the window, not learning to read but soothing myself with food. In college I gained and lost fifty pounds—twice. Post college, I usually weighed between five to fifteen pounds more than I should have. But despite being a little curvy, I had an active love life. However, I viewed every man in my life as a happy accident. Although generally satisfied with my appearance, I never felt particularly attractive to the opposite sex.

Conversely, I've always been completely comfortable in my own skin and never the least bit insecure in intimate situations. Looking good naked was never my issue. While my inner hottie thrived in private, my public, outer hottie lacked confidence.

After completing the Fifteen Pounds to Menopause Diet, I gave away my entire wardrobe. Some of my clothes, like blue jeans, were replaced twice. A pal at work, a wonderful woman also named Joanna, told me I had great legs and should stop wearing long, flowing skirts and instead start wearing clothes that showed off my assets.

Although I'd been the same size in previous periods of my life, I hadn't known how to dress myself. Now, I did. That fall I discovered the pencil skirt, a slim, curve- hugging piece of clothing that reaches the knee and looks good on almost everyone. There's nothing comparable to make a girl feel attractive. I walked around the office halls in my pencil skirts and sweaters feeling like a sexy secretary, circa a 1950s movie—think Marilyn

Monroe, Betty Grable, and Lauren Bacall in *How to Marry a Millionaire.* I began noticing men looking at me as I walked down the streets. This was wonderful and fun, but somehow it never fully hit me until Rick got squirrelly with me. His moment of embarrassment became my moment of truth.

This year, my outer hottie finally emerged. The week I had my first date with my ex-husband, Harry, whom I met in the laundry room of our building, I also had five blind dates with other men I met through personal ads. Harry was the only one of the six to ask for a second date. I also had six first dates this year. Everyone except Sam, the Iranian, wanted to see me again. My outer hottie is here to stay, and I'm going to embrace it and enjoy myself. Goodness knows, I'm trying.

KISS OF DEATH

Many of the men posting personal ads on the Internet state they're looking for intelligent women. Based on my experience, I believe if the ads were truthful they'd read, "Looking for a woman to make fifteen minutes of interesting small talk before I sleep with her." When men comment that I'm smart, chances are the romance is about to end or will never get started. Regardless of what men say, most are not looking for smart women. I don't think the men are lying; I just think they're deluding themselves.

Everyone knows brilliant women who are in relationships, but intelligence doesn't seem to be the main attraction even if men appreciate this quality and would be dissatisfied with women who aren't bright. I know members of the opposite sex who are completely enamored with their partners, but I've never heard one comment on their beloved's intelligence. They comment on women's bodies, sweetness, kindness, and generosity, or they praise their talents. They don't comment on their mate's intelligence when romance is involved.

When I mentioned this to my Uncle Jon, he disagreed, explaining that prior to their marriage, my father spoke highly of my mother's intelligence.

I replied, "Yes, that was in1956. Has anyone said it since?" There was dead silence on the other end of the line.

In the mid-nineties, I attended the wedding of an odd couple. The bride was petite, while her tall groom weighed at least three hundred pounds and towered over her. Fifteen years her senior, he came from an

Italian immigrant family, while her parents had emigrated from Mainland China. Everyone who knew this couple understood that the bride had pushed the relationship forward, and, left to his own devices, the groom would never have asked for a first date.

Standing in the vestibule of the church before the ceremony, I overheard several Italian matriarchs in pre-wedding chatter. The ladies made the same comment to each other ("She's so smart"), but didn't say much else about the bride. When listening to this refrain, it struck me: they didn't like her at all—not because intelligence wasn't respected but because it was a devalued commodity in a bride. If the Italian matrons had liked her, they might have commented on her looks, warmth, humor, cooking skills, or devotion to the groom—anything but her intelligence. They seemed to be speaking in code, as if saying, "Why is he marrying this woman? She's smart, but not much else." These tough Italian ladies didn't seem to understand why the groom would marry someone whose only perceived virtue was her intelligence. They knew men don't do that. They understood what makes men tick.

I had an eye opening experience at the nursing home where I'm employed while participating in a resident-care conference. During these meetings, the various providers give progress reports and hash out pertinent care issues. Without thinking about it, I commented that a patient was *non compos mentis* (a common Latin term meaning not sane.) One of the three male doctors at the meeting asked what the phrase meant. Another questioned if I was making fun of them. Making fun by using Latin with doctors? Shocked by their comment, I didn't know how to respond, except to reply sarcastically, "Yes, I'm making fun of you."

Over time, I've learned that when a man tells me I'm smart, it's the romantic equivalent of the kiss of death. It's happened three times in less than a year. First, after a promising initial date last December, the man stated he wanted to see me again. A week later, he informed me he'd changed his mind and preferred to hang out and go to the movies with me, but he didn't want to get involved romantically. In the same breath, he mentioned how smart I was. Next, the crazy Buddhist, Llama Gensho, commented on my intelligence as he dumped me. I met the third guy through a personal ad. On his invitation via e-mail, I'd called him. We talked for over an hour, and it seemed as if things were going smoothly until the end of the conversation when my potential Romeo said, "How nice it is to talk to an intelligent woman." He then asked for my phone number. Silly me, I actually believed he might call. My man-speak skills had failed me temporarily. Had they been operative, I'd have known when he said he enjoyed speaking to an intelligent woman, he meant, "You scare me to death. I'll never ask you out, and this is the only way I know of to get off the phone."

Here's a true confession: At thirteen years old, I yearned to be a genius. I didn't believe any demonstrable, genius-like talents were necessary and instead hoped I might be one based solely on intelligence. It's not a bad dream as stupid adolescent fantasies go.

I've recently tried to understand my secret wish, and I'm beginning to grasp its meaning. I often joke that I've burned all the photographs of myself at thirteen. Unless you're Brook Shields, thirteen isn't usually a girl's most attractive age. It was abominable for me. By the time I turned eleven, my mother had completely abdicated all responsibility for helping me buy clothes and instead handed me some cash and sent me shopping alone. I bought whatever fit—not a pretty sight. Mom never provided any lessons in Shopping 101, so I didn't know you could be a consistent size until I was twenty. In addition, my hair became frizzy, and I was so ungainly that I literally walked into walls.

But at thirteen, an amazing teacher began to nurture me. Mrs. Flynn helped change my self-concept. She was the stuff of myths and movie-of-the-week weepies. Teachers like her deserve their own monument—maybe a Mount Rushmore for educators. With only a little encouragement and positive feedback, Mrs. Flynn helped change how I thought of myself. Much of her feedback involved my brainpower. At forty-five, I'm still in contact with her.

It's easy now to see that my desire to be a genius was linked to Mrs. Flynn's positive reinforcement. Without the maturity at the time to understand my impulse, I may have felt that being exceptionally smart could help me find a comfortable place in the world, a place where you didn't need to be pretty and where it was okay to have other talents. A place where it was all right to slam into walls without warning. I hoped someone would give me a clue about my genius-hood, a small tidbit I could cling to, but it never happened. Nevertheless, I managed to grow up and feel good about myself for more reality-based reasons. Had I known that being smart would serve as extra-strength man repellent, I'd never have engaged in that particular fantasy.

In films, it's considered romantic for a woman to have a man who "got away," but it's not romantic at all in reality. I know—Alan got away from me. Of all the men who've passed through my life, he's the only one with whom the experience feels incomplete, even after eighteen years. We spent three enchanting days together in Boston in 1988, and then he continued his travels and returned home to Australia. Life isn't fair, but I'm glad I had three days with him. It was like *Roman Holiday*—brief but deeply felt.

Alan is the exception to my anti-intelligence theory. After his visit I could barely function and blew off all my plans for the day, going to the movies instead. Looking back, I'm glad that at least *once* my brains were part of the main attraction and not a harbinger of romantic death rays.

So, where does that leave a brainy, mouthy girl like me? Even though I've recently discovered my outer hottie, it's still demoralizing when doctors mock my vocabulary. I'm not sure how to reconcile these opposing forces, one that attracts and another that seems to terrorize men. I now know I can try to change my behavior, but I can't change my fundamental nature. And if I tried to be less of whatever intimidates men, the truth would come out eventually. There aren't many movies that feature a female protagonist in which intelligence alone is central to the character, except perhaps in films made from Jane Austen novels, like Elizabeth Bennet in *Pride and Prejudice.* In other films the characters are more likely to be smart *and* a babe, like Julia Roberts in *Erin Brocovich*, where the title character is clearly whip smart, but also superstar sexy. I'm aging well, but not that well.

My niece, Juliet, recently had her bat mitzvah. She *is* truly beautiful at age thirteen. Sometimes at the parties for bat or bar mitzvahs, there's a candle lighting ceremony. The bar/bat mitzvah child calls thirteen people (or groups of people) who are meaningful to him or her to the front of the room to light a candle. When Juliet called on me, she said many kind things, including a comment about my optimism. I was surprised and touched that she perceives me this way. Now I have an opportunity to embody her perception of me by holding on to the belief that there is someone in the dating universe who will be attracted to me just as I am. It's happened at least once, eighteen years ago, and it could happen again. I'll be sure to tell my beautiful niece.

DREAMLAND ENCOURAGEMENT

Last night's dream has stayed with me since I woke up. It has hovered in my consciousness throughout the day, first at synagogue, where I intended to focus on loftier matters, then at lunch with friends when it kept popping into my head at odd moments, then at the video and drugstores where it seemed to affect my ability to make correct change, and finally sitting on my couch during the evening, trying unsuccessfully to distract myself with a movie. The dream lingers, and I'm wondering what it's supposed to mean.

The dream started at a wedding—my wedding. Guests lined up outside a modest wedding chapel waiting to enter. Most of them were dressed in t-shirts and casual weekend clothes, as if they were about to rake leaves instead of witness the beginning of a marriage. If anyone ever showed up at a wedding of mine dressed like that, I'd probably nurse my indignation and resentment well past a ten-year anniversary. So, I knew immediately that the dream was out of synch with everyday reality and seemed to be about some laid-back version of my high-strung self.

The dream segued into a small room inside the chapel used by the bridal party to prepare for nuptials. I could sense my betrothed, but I couldn't see him. Two or three chapel employees were also in the room. My wedding dress had been folded in two and slung over the top of a dresser. Seeing the dress, I thought, "This is going to be a no-fuss affair." In my waking life, I assume that my second wedding, the one I envision in my head from time to time, won't be a formal shindig like the first one.

But I'd never sling a wedding dress anywhere. After noticing the dress, I asked the chapel staff to give the groom and me a moment alone.

At that moment, the scene shifted, and my fiancé and I were curled up together on a bed, which hadn't been in the room before. The object of my affection had blond hair, fresh-butter blond, the type you usually don't see on grown men. I'm not particularly attracted to blonds, but he had warm features and would be considered attractive by any reasonable standard. My fiancé lay on his back with me draped over and facing him. I noticed that his hand hung off the bed and held a cigarette. Surprised, I calmly commented, "Oh, you're a smoker," clearly noticing this for the first time. I teased, "Do you know how many first dates I've refused because the guy smoked?" It was a rhetorical question, and the smoking wasn't a deal breaker.

With my first marriage, or more accurately, my non-dreamland marriage, after making our vows, I discovered that my husband, Harry, smoked one cigarette a day. We'd dated for four years before marrying, and I'd never seen him smoke a cigarette in all that time. I was deeply upset by this revelation even though it was only one cigarette. So, it seemed I had gone from real-world distress to dream-world equanimity about the smoking issue.

Next in the dream, my fiancé, in the same loving tones with which we'd discussed his smoking, told me he was gay. We were cuddling in this moment, not fighting. But nothing seemed to change our intention to get married. I replied, "You know what this means? No more men for you." My fiancé calmly accepted my ultimatum. Just as with the smoking, there was no debate. We were who we were, and we were about to get married. My waking life is never this simple and easy.

The end of my dream reminded me of one of the final scenes in *The Eternal Sunshine of the Spotless Mind*. At the conclusion of the film, Kate Winslet lists all of her faults to Jim Carey, with whom she's had a tumultuous romance. He listens and then firmly and calmly accepts her. I love this movie.

Despite the unexpected issues, my dream conveyed, more than anything else, a great closeness between us. My fiancé was going to give up men, and I was going to live with his smoking. The mood of the dream was so piercingly intimate that it woke me. Now I can't get it off my mind or figure out what I'm supposed to learn from it.

I would never become involved with a gay smoker. Either issue would be out of the question. Although I've heard of women who have made this choice, intentionally marrying a gay man would be a surefire recipe for untold complications and heartache for me, and the smoking would drive me crazy. Yet the most striking part of the dream wasn't the smoking or homosexuality, but rather how unimportant these matters were in the presence of the warmth and love. After the dream haunted me all day, the only conclusion I could draw was that I need to be more open to love, even if it comes in unexpected forms.

But how much more open? If they gave out awards for diversity in dating, I'd win it this year. I became involved with someone who believed he was a Buddhist priest, and who also dressed like one. I've gone out with an orthodox Jew and with men of three different ethnicities—Black, Caucasian, and Middle Eastern. In addition, I had one date with someone who had a severe birth defect, which I knew about before I met him. One of my dates would have been an excellent candidate for gastric bypass surgery (I also knew he was fat before we went out), and two of the guys were so short, I would have hovered over them in heels, like every woman Tom Cruise has ever been photographed with. One of the men I dated had a PhD, at least two had master's degrees, and one had never attended college. I'm not sure how much wider to cast my dating net, short of trolling in bars or hiking up my skirts on street corners.

If I weren't a Jew and instead worshipped the Greek gods, I'd shake my fist at Hypnos, the god of sleep, and yell, "What more do you want from me? Do you really want me to date *gay chain smokers*?" Even by my ridiculously broad standards, that's asking too much.

Or maybe I've got it all wrong. Maybe instead of providing redirection, the dream is a message of encouragement. Perhaps it's implying that I don't know where I'll find love; it might come from an unexpected quarter. It might be outside the box, something I couldn't predict. Possibly the dream isn't telling me to change my behavior at all. Maybe it's urging me to relax, to keep the faith, and is letting me know, "Look, this is going to happen, just not the way you think it will." Now there's a message I could embrace. I only hope it's true.

Joanna J. Charnas

DATING A SOCIOPATH: NO HARM DONE

When you're dating, it's easy to be idealistic and believe you're going to hold out for true love, but hormones and the shadow of countless nights alone are powerful influences. I know what it feels like to have an instant connection with someone—I've experienced that feeling several times. It's nothing short of magical. Once you've felt those emotions and they've been reciprocated, it's difficult to imagine accepting anything less. However when some seemingly nice guy runs his fingers through the curls at the back of my collar and slowly rubs my neck, instinct takes over. I'm less likely to think, "You are not at all like R., who made me glow every time he walked into the room." I'm more likely to say, "Oh, please, a little to the left." At those moments, my thoughts usually run something like this: *Thank God you find me attractive; Thank God I find you attractive; Thank God you speak standard English and use the word "symbiotic" correctly in a sentence*; or sometimes, just *Thank God you're not a sociopath.* Reason fails me during these moments, and I turn into your basic primal sludge.

Last week, I might have dated a sociopath. I remain unnerved by the encounter. All of the men whom I'd dated earlier this year, except one, was forty or younger. I hadn't intended to date younger men—things just evolved that way. So, I decided to see if there were any younger men purposely looking for an older woman on the dating sites I frequented. It would be a new adventure.

Jake had lived in San Diego for seven months and told me he found the younger women here "shallow." This wasn't the first time I'd heard this, so I believed him. He informed me he found older women attractive, and I believed that too. At thirty, Jake was a full sixteen years younger than me.

Our first date went well, and we had our second date two days later on a Monday. The date involved some major nooky on my couch, interaction so heated I needed to say more than once, "I just can't sleep with you on the second date." During both dates, Jake frequently stated his intention to see me again and his desire to start a serious relationship. He said, "We're going to have so much fun together."

He lied. By Tuesday, I knew something was wrong. Jake had made all kinds of noises about seeing me again before I departed for a four-day weekend over the Christmas holiday, but he hadn't reached out to me for the first time since we began talking five days ago. My reaction to his lack of contact most accurately could be described as a two-and-a-half-day anxiety attack. I lost my appetite, couldn't sleep, and was a nervous wreck. I thought I'd lost my mind. I was appalled by what I interpreted as my own neediness. This was no way to celebrate the holiday season.

By Thursday, I assumed I wouldn't be hearing from Jake again. I went back online, where I'd seen his personal add, looking for clues to his change of heart. That's when I discovered he'd posted eight or nine personal ads in December, all seeking *different kinds* of woman. He sought *a fit black beauty, a fun female with a wild side, a single black female for friendship/relationship, a stoner girlfriend, a sexy older female*, etcetera, ad nauseam.

I could easily identify Jake as the author of all the postings because he always described himself in the same manner: "six foot two, one hundred sixty-five pounds" (very skinny), "with blue eyes." He consistently stated his interests as some variation of "movies, indie films, art, bonfires (bonfires?), dive bars, cards, camping, and dancing," among others.

I understand the logic of casting a broad net, but this was creepy. Stating a distinct preference for vastly different kinds of women as if each was specifically and exclusively what he was looking for was deceitful. Moreover, none of the ads had overlapping criteria. For example, the ad seeking older women made no mention of the pot, and the ad looking for an African American woman didn't cite an age preference. Jake was clever in his deception.

I talked to Uncle Jon about the array of postings and marveled at the obviousness of Jake's ploy. "Didn't he know that if I met him this way, I'd probably discover *all* the postings and figure out what he was up to?" I whined.

"He doesn't care," Jon replied, and he was right. That's what made Jake a sociopath—the not caring.

When I realized Jake was a heel whose only motivation seemed to be to get me into bed quickly, I felt much better about my two-and-a-half days of insanity. Instead of feeling needy, I chalked up my extended anxiety attack to good instincts. I'd known something was terribly wrong, but I'd required few days to figure out the details. Romantic comedies in which the themes revolve around a lie are often charming, like *While You Were Sleeping* or *The Truth About Cats and Dogs.* In reality, lies and romance don't mix and only serve as minefields for disappointment and pain.

The downside of this romantic quest is that I dated someone who turned out to be a manipulative jerk, but with no real harm done. The upside is that I had major fun on both dates and in particular during the two-hour romp on my couch. Although I may have been stupid enough to go out with a sociopath, the limits and boundaries I set with Jake (including keeping my pants on) served me well. All the good sense I've tried to apply while dating this year appears to have taken hold, because whatever this guy wanted, it took only two dates for him to realize he wasn't going to get it from me.

I suspect the only honest thing Jake said to me was that I have "beautiful skin." People have admired my skin for my entire adult life, including earlier this year when Llama Gensho approached me with this line. Total strangers in ladies' rooms frequently feel compelled to praise it, the way you might compliment a beautiful baby in the supermarket. But everything else that came out of Jake's mouth was probably some form of a lie. It seems like such a waste of energy to work so diligently at being duplicitous, and the social worker in me can't help wondering what truth Jake was hiding.

The truth for me, which is always difficult to acknowledge when a part of me feels good, is that something was missing with Jake. I enjoyed myself with him but only in a superficial way. The thought passed through my mind, as we pawed each other on the couch, that Jake would be pleasant to have around, but not much more.

In general, I've had a good year dating. Of the nine men I've gone out with, seven asked for second dates—a remarkably high rate for a middle-aged late bloomer. I've had a lot of ups and downs this year, but I've also had more fun than I experienced in the previous three post-divorce years combined. Since I won't be seeing the sociopath again, I guess I have another shot at true love. More than ever, I believe I'm ready for it.

THE NEW GUY

You don't always know when you're experiencing burnout until you're hip deep in its muck. You also don't comprehend how completely addicting Internet dating is until you're hooked. So if you find yourself burned out from Internet dating, as I did, the prudent thing is to give it a rest. Although I planned to take a break from Internet dating, I'd become too addicted to stop. It didn't matter that I was emotionally exhausted from too many blind dates. Which is when Simon entered my life.

I met Simon on an Internet dating site. When we first spoke on the phone, he asked if I'd meet him that evening at a party given in honor of a couple of his friends. Simon explained that his schedule was booked for the rest of the week, but he wanted to meet me right away. The party started in mid-afternoon, and assuming I wouldn't be enslaved and forced into the sex trade, I agreed to rendezvous at his friends' house late in the afternoon. I planned to stay for an hour, two at most—just long enough to get acquainted with Simon. Instead, I remained at the party five and a half hours and didn't leave until after 10:00 p.m.

Simon's friends were down to earth, easy to talk to, and lovely. I spent my time at this party alternately chatting with Simon and talking to his buddies, who were mostly social service providers or teachers.

To my surprise, Simon didn't look remotely like the photograph he'd posted on his personal ad. I could have plowed into him in the supermarket and never guessed he was the person whose ad I'd answered, but I didn't care. Simon was warm, bright, and seemed caring. Similarly entranced by his great group of friends, I would have happily dated every man at the party.

Simon's parting words on Saturday night had been about his desire to see me the next weekend. He e-mailed me twice after the party but never actually asked me out. I tried to keep my responses light and positive although I couldn't understand why he never made plans with me. I thought to myself, *Just pick up the damn phone and ask me out!* Instead, he seemed to slip into the cyber void.

When I thought I'd never see Simon again, I became unglued. Many sugary substances were consumed. I came home from work every night, went to bed, pulled the covers up to my nose, summoned the cat, and watched hours of mindless television. I was so disappointed that he hadn't called by Friday, I spent forty-five minutes answering a phone survey simply to have a focused human interaction.

By Saturday, after I'd given up on hearing from him, Simon called to ask me out that night. Our date started at 6:00 p.m. in a cheap restaurant that served great sushi and ended at 2:00 a.m. down the block at a coffee shop with deep couches. Partway through the evening, Simon confessed, "This is one of the best dates I've ever had."

Burned out, jaded, and generally insensitive from too much dating, I responded, "Is that a line?"

Not fazed by my rudeness, he answered, "If it is, it's true."

I had become unaccustomed to sincere, complimentary men in the past year. I didn't want the date to end. It didn't until the coffee shop closed and Simon kissed me goodnight on the sidewalk.

All year, I'd been pining for some old-fashioned wooing. The ups and downs of months of whirlwind dating had left me yearning for sincere validation that didn't include immediately trying to get into my underwear. I found myself happily spaced out the next day. That afternoon, Simon called to say he'd had a great time the night before. This would have been more than enough validation for me. Finally—someone who liked me and had good manners. But then he surprised me by suggesting we meet for dinner again that night. I'd hoped this was the start of something good, and I got my wish.

For weeks after we began dating, I refused to call Simon by his name when I talked about him to my friends and family. Instead I referred to him exclusively as "the new guy." I only revealed his name, at their insistence, after a month of avoidance. Superstitious, I feared if I released his name to anyone, I'd doom the relationship. Pretending he was an anonymous male specimen made me feel less likely to tempt fate into jerking him away from me.

Simon's personal ad stated that he wanted to do "fun things," and we embarked on a series of them with gusto. He took me all over San Diego County on adventures. We went to community fairs, music festivals, open-air theater, and free movies in the park. We enjoyed meandering walks together and explored different dives where I tried foods I'd never eaten before. He even taught me how to boogie board. It was heaven.

He took me on my second trip to Disneyland. After my first trip a couple of years earlier, I'd thought, "Well that was interesting, but I never need to do it again." I'd purposely screened out all the men whose personal ads said they loved Disneyland. When six months into the relationship Simon asked me to spend a day there with him, I thought, why not? I hoped he could make the experience fresh and exciting. I had so much fun, at the end of the visit I bought a season's pass.

I knew Simon was a keeper when he told me he had seen the film *Guernica.* This movie is about the infamous bombing during the Spanish Civil War, memorialized forever by Picasso's masterpiece depicting the same event. No one I'd met before had seen the movie. His familiarity with this mostly unknown film gave me hope that we shared similar sensibilities. Maybe I'd finally met a man who might enjoy some of the obscure independent films I loved and that were a vital part of my life. I told him my hero since adolescence—the great *Life* photographer, all around Renaissance man, and director of *Shaft*—had died shortly after we began dating. Simon admired Gordon Parks' photographs and also knew he'd directed *Shaft*. His familiarity with my beloved hero was deeply meaningful to me.

Meeting Simon's family sealed the deal. When I'd trolled for men on the Internet, I'd hoped to find a mate who had children since there's a long, successful history of stepmothers in my family. Simon didn't have children—he had an entire clan. Simon's mother was one of seven siblings in a Jewish family who moved from Alabama in the early 1960s. His mother's generation all had southern drawls and charm, embodying the best of both Jewish and southern cultures. Once you met a family member, from that point on he or she always hugged and kissed you in greeting.

I met Simon's entire family for the first time a couple of months after we began dating. I'd been invited to their annual Passover gathering. By this time, I'd stopped going to New York for Passover because my great aunt and uncle, increasingly frail, had downsized their Seder to immediate family, mostly children and grandchildren. Even though we'd only been dating briefly, Simon's family embraced me and treated me like one of their own. Several of his first cousins approached me at the dinner break and inquired if I felt overwhelmed. To the contrary, I felt relaxed and was completely smitten. It was all so much better than what I'd wanted. I realized I'd been dreaming small.

After our fifth date, I informed Simon that I have a chronic illness. I told him the truth—that I lead a normal life, but I have limitations and need a lot of down time. He barely blinked, saying if I became sick, he'd come to my home and feed me. True to his word, two months later when I contracted food poisoning and couldn't keep anything down, he brought me rice, chicken, and meringue cookies—the latter, he explained, was so I'd have something sweet.

Within a few months of dating, our friends, family, and colleagues began to ask each of us if we were thinking about getting married. This seemed premature, but I understood that implicit in their questions was their recognition of the growing seriousness of our relationship. I felt ambivalent about marriage. I'd been married before and didn't need to marry again. The questions freaked Simon out. I reassured him that I didn't care if we got married, but my reassurances didn't calm him. By his mid-twenties, Simon's mother had married his third stepfather, and I assumed all of those marriages left him wary of the institution. I didn't take Simon's response to the idea of marriage personally. I didn't need to marry him. We lived fewer than two miles apart, which allowed for spontaneity without constraint.

Looking back on my year of whirlwind dating that preceded meeting Simon, I sometimes question my judgment. I often think I shouldn't have become involved with Lama Gensho. Despite our initial intense connection, the relationship was never going to last, even if he hadn't gotten grumpy and dumped me. And despite my faith and love for my orthodox congregation, I'm probably not capable of maintaining an orthodox home, which Saul, whom I dated three times, needed. I've struggled to understand the swells and drifts of my psyche that led me to believe those relationships might work.

Now, I think I understand. When I divorced my husband, I believed with absolute certainty there would be at least one more significant love in my future. I refused to think my love life was completely over despite the multi-year dry spell that immediately followed the divorce. Even when profoundly discouraged, I never relinquished this belief. I might view my year of dating choices as unrealistic and naïve if I were a more negative person, but I prefer to look back on the year and believe all that hope was born of optimism as much as naiveté. Every time I met someone with the qualities I sought, I applied my optimistic nature to each situation, regardless of the larger realities.

At a former employer's request, I once took a lengthy and expensive test to identify my strengths in the workplace. Of over one hundred sixty options, one of my identified, top five strengths was "positivity." One of my colleagues recently told me she liked working with me because I'm "so positive." If I hadn't been inherently optimistic while dating, the emotional strain of meeting numerous men and laying myself bare for repeated evaluation and rejection or acceptance would have been too hard on me. Instead, I saw the best in every situation.

My widowed aunt once told me that she thinks relationships "last as long as they last." Sometimes they last twenty-five years, like her marriage to my uncle, and sometimes they last six months, like the relationship she'd just ended. I saw the wisdom of her philosophy. When I first met Simon, like many of the guys I'd dated in the previous year, he inquired what I wanted from a relationship. I told him I wanted a long-term, committed relationship, but that I didn't care if we lived together or were married.

Simon liked to spot older couples in public and point them out to me. Sometimes it was a set-up for a joke. He'd see a stooped, gray-haired couple and say, "That's us in three years." More often, he'd see an elderly couple and whisper, "That's us in thirty years." I hope so, but as my aunt advised, it lasts as long as it lasts. I can live with that.

MOVING ON IN STYLE

Collette said it best. "What remains to be said about a passionate love affair? It can be told in three lines: *He* loved me, I loved *Him*. *His* presence obliterated all other presences. We were happy. Then *He* stopped loving me, and I suffered."[1] Simon didn't cease to love me, but I broke up with him because I realized he'd never loved me enough. Occasionally, I wonder if he loved me at all. I suffered, anyway, so it amounts to the same thing. There's a long story that led me to this conclusion, but the story is just detail.

Simon's personal ad stated he sought a woman for fun activities. True to his word, we enjoyed innumerable adventures during our five-year relationship. He loved planning, executing, and being the ringmaster of all our large and small forays. But after I broke up with him, I recognized that fun was mostly what he had to offer. He didn't possess deeper feelings. Although often sweet and kind, he wasn't consistently either. A hothead, he sometimes yelled when upset. I couldn't tolerate the yelling despite the fact that it never turned to abuse. Unfortunately, Simon's commitment to changing this behavior vacillated.

Simon often declared he wanted to grow old with me yet didn't adequately demonstrate the behaviors my other serious boyfriends had. We only spent one night a week actually sleeping together even though we lived two miles apart. After spending an evening together, one of us usually got into our car and drove home. He wanted this arrangement, and I'm so independent, it wasn't a major issue for me. But after the breakup, I reflected on it. Every other guy who'd wanted a future with me desired the intimacy of shared slumber. There were four of those men, and they'd made their feelings clear by spending every night with me, something each of them initiated. They didn't joke about being wobbly, gray, old people together and then hug me goodnight at my front door. I wasn't angry about this, just dumbfounded that it took me so long to put my foot down. Being an eternal optimist definitely has its disadvantages.

So, at fifty, I found myself single again. I might have felt terrible, but my waves of sadness, anger, grief, and loss never lasted longer than an afternoon or evening. There were no crying jags after my breakup with Simon, and I required only one emergency call to Uncle Jon for kindness, support, and the warmth of his special brand of avuncular love. During this breakup, I *did not* fall into a swamp of morose emotions, like Jon Favreau in *Swingers*. Although Jon's character ends the relationship with his girlfriend, six months later he still feels so bad, he appears clinically depressed. I was sad but fine.

This breakup was easy compared to my divorce, after which I wept two or three times a day for four months. The crying jags ended abruptly on September 11, 2001, four months to the day after my ex-husband moved out. My horror and grief at our national tragedy superseded my personal distress, and I snapped out of it. After the terrorist attacks, I moved on to less dramatic manifestations of sadness. But I didn't feel like myself again for another year.

I had dinner with Dave about a month and a half after the breakup with Simon. Dave, one of the Eight Men Who Love Me, had experienced a slump, and I'd been in a slump (the long story), so we hadn't seen each other for several months. As I told him about the breakup, I realized I'd changed. Instead of feeling like a failure for never having the long-term relationship of my dreams, it dawned on me that I thought of myself as a serial monogamist—not precisely what I wanted, but it didn't feel bad, either.

I reminded myself that I'm a late bloomer and may not have reached my full romantic potential yet. If there were an award for the latest of late bloomers, I would be Grand Champion Supreme.

There are members of my father's family who live to be at least ninety and often look ten years younger than their age. People consistently expressed shock when they learned my age. They always asked me how I achieved my youthful appearance. I gave full credit to my freaky genetics as well as an entire adulthood of sun avoidance. In an era of age-defying makeup rituals and increasingly popular plastic surgery, I felt as though I'd won an award. This genetic lottery prize helped me accept being single again. I was fifty disguised as a forty-year-old, an advantage in our youth-obsessed culture.

On the locked psych ward where I've worked for the past few years, I often talk to young service members in the Army, Marines, or Navy who have recently experienced their first manic episode or psychotic break. They often question their extreme misfortune. These kids break my heart. All I can tell them is that they're right—life is unfair, and they have every reason to feel angry and sad about the hand they were dealt. I try to help them come to terms with their illnesses to the best of my limited ability.

I didn't equate one person's major mental illness with another person's inability to find a soul mate, but I wanted to practice what I preached about accepting life's struggles. So, I didn't question why I hadn't found lasting romantic love. I accepted it as my fate. I had at least one friend who fell madly in love with her second husband in her mid-seventies, and I was deeply encouraged by her story. I hoped I might also find a genuine and lasting love later in life.

Shortly after my breakup with Simon, I went to DSW (Designer Shoe Warehouse) to buy shoes for work. I found what I wanted and then wandered to the back of the store to the sales racks, a dangerous place where wild designer shoes were drastically marked down. All manner of colorful, shiny, spiky footwear was displayed there. It was an especially dangerous place for a middle-aged, newly single woman with the blues. In these racks, I discovered black patent leather Joan & David ankle boots. They weren't exactly boots, but rather, they resembled high-end hooker shoes. Beautiful and sleek, they fit perfectly. I resisted them. I left the store without the shoes, even though they were marked an additional thirty percent off the reduced price. Feeling virtuous, I loaded my more sensible purchases into my car and drove away.

At work, I told several friends about my trip to DSW and the beautiful shoes I'd left behind. I called them "my dominatrix shoes." Two friends urged me to go back and grab them, as if they were sending me on a Special Forces mission. Another friend asked, "Why do you need dominatrix shoes?" I hedged, explaining that they weren't actually dominatrix shoes.

After two days of black patent leather on my mind, I returned to DSW to buy them. I decided if I was meant to own them, they would be there waiting for me to rescue them.

When I arrived at DSW, I found the shoes, as beautiful and shiny as I remembered. I asked a stylishly dressed young woman if she thought my dominatrix boots (not the term I used at that moment) would look good with a black pencil skirt. She answered affirmatively, sized me up, and replied slowly, "Those look good."

Why did I need a pair of black patent leather Joan & David almost-ankle boots/almost-dominatrix shoes? Because at fifty, I was single again. I wanted to look hot, sexy, and a little dangerous. The shoes made me feel in control of my fate. When I brought my frivolous purchase home, I slipped on my black pencil skirt and thought to myself, "Baby doll, you are good to go."

And once again, I was.

[1] Colette, Robert Phelps. 1983. *The collected stories of Colette*. New York: Farrar, Straus, Giroux.

BIG CHANGES: 2012

If anyone had predicted the changes I'd experience in my love life during the past year, I'd have bet large sums of money that they were wrong. I've dated so many men this year, I've begun to refer to them by number: One, Two, Three, and Four. My friend Arnie has received a blow-by-blow account of every romantic up and down I've experienced. He observed that numbering the men was dehumanizing, but when we discussed the last man I dated, we agreed that man hadn't been sufficiently significant to merit a whole number. Arnie dubbed him Four Point One, which I thought apt.

Right after my breakup with Simon, I needed a breather. My first venture back into dating took place almost a year after I'd last seen Simon. At a barbeque for middle-age Jewish singles, a man I'd chatted with over burgers gave me his number and asked me to call him. He seemed like a nice guy who deserved a chance, but half an hour into the date, I wanted to end it. He mostly talked about himself and then asked me if I was prone to anxiety. I laughed and replied, "Of course, I am." He offered to help me "fix that." I've been diagnosed with mild General Anxiety Disorder, but I don't want anyone to offer to fix me on the first date, or ever. I gave this man an hour of my life and then left.

Shortly after that date, things began to change. At the end of the previous year, a man in my social circle (Number One) had flirted with me and mentioned taking me for a ride up the coast in his convertible, but he never asked me out. In July, without much thought, I told Number One I still wanted a ride. By August, he'd offered to take me for a drive, but I wasn't sure we were on a date until he greeted me with an energetic kiss. We drove to a beautiful state park, where he grabbed me almost at once and began to nuzzle me in places that hadn't had human contact for a year. I mentioned that there were other people around and suggested we move somewhere private. I imagined hapless tourists complaining that they'd visited a state park and found old people making out.

Number One and I discovered we possessed chemistry that verged on porn, but after two months, I sensed that although he was fun to romp with both indoors and out, one didn't cut it as boyfriend material. He agreed with my assessment, so we broke up.

About a month later, One intimated that he didn't want our relationship to end, and I agreed to see him whenever we had the urge. "Friends-with-benefits" gets a bad rap and conjures up images of crass relationships, as in the movie *Bridesmaids*, where people are uncaring and unloving, but our relationship made me feel as though I'd entered a sophisticated French movie, sizzling hot while also fundamentally cool, resembling *Last Tango In Paris* without the sexual sadism. I knew One wouldn't be around too often, so I told him I planned to date other people, but neither of us expected me to become involved with someone else so soon.

Number Two entered my life a few weeks later as a blind date set up by a friend of a friend. The woman joined a small dinner party I gave on my fifty-second birthday. She informed me she had a colleague who wanted a romantic relationship, showed me his photo, and told me to google him since he was prominent in his field. Excited and encouraged, I gave her my phone number. Later on, after googling him, I discovered he didn't look like the handsome, middle-aged man whose photo I'd been shown. He instead appeared much older. When he called me a couple of weeks later, we clearly had many common interests and were able to engage in lively repartee, so I agreed to a coffee date.

When we first met, Two appeared fifteen to twenty years older than me. He wore khaki slacks, good loafers, and a tasteful sweater, usually cashmere. He was Italian, and I felt as if I were dating *The Godfather*. Number Two dated as though it was 1965. He always took me out to eat and sometimes to a movie, or we would watch a DVD after dinner, and then he wanted to have sex. We saw each other about once a week. He never left one date without scheduling the next one, but rarely spoke to me in between. I might have suspected he was married or otherwise attached, but another friend knew him too, and confirmed his single status. Two informed me the photo I'd seen was fifteen years old. He refused to let me see him naked or tell me his age. Usually I can't see much without glasses, but since we slept together, I could reasonably assess what he might look like with the lights and my glasses on. His vanity was ridiculous. The week before we broke up, without any prompting from me, Two disclosed that he was seventy-one. I would have never intentionally dated someone that much older, but I enjoyed his company, and the old guy was a stud.

After a couple of months, Two and I were treading water. I enjoyed his dating rituals, but I wanted more. Devastated when one of my patients committed suicide, I called him for support but couldn't reach him. I didn't want to trivialize the patient's death with a phone message, so I never left one. When I told him the next day about her suicide, he made no utterances of empathy or kindness. A day later, during a rare phone call when I expressed concern that we weren't in sync, he told me he didn't want to discuss this issue on the phone. Instead, he text messaged me three days later to inform me that we didn't want the same things, and he broke up with me.

Number One had been eager to continue seeing me while I dated Two and checked in with me every couple of weeks to see if we were still an item. I told him I didn't want to date (and sleep with) both of them at once. In response, he asked repeatedly to let him know if it didn't work out, and I assured him I would. His eagerness to reconnect with me resulted in one of the quickest rebounds known in middle-age womanhood. Within less than twenty hours of being dumped via text message, I was whizzing around in One's convertible. I explained my week had been terrible, including losing a patient to suicide and being dumped. By the end of our date, I felt immensely better. Nevertheless, I still experienced the sting of being dumped and the sadness that a relationship with Two didn't develop into anything meaningful. I learned that one relationship may not necessarily impact another. I had no idea I could feel such oppositional feelings or that my love life could be so complex and rich. I continued to see One while I wasn't dating anyone else.

Less than two weeks later, as I slowly recovered from the shock of being dumped via text message, I went to my very first movie meet-up and met Number Three. Meet-ups are social gatherings of groups of people, mostly strangers, with common interests. There are thousands of them in San Diego. I'd been meaning to go to a movie meet-up for a year, but hadn't gotten around to it. It seemed like a good antidote to my newly single state. About sixty people attended the meet-up, most of whom stood talking to each other before the movie started. I have a form of low blood pressure that often makes it hard for me to stand for extended periods of time. So, as everyone else stood and schmoozed, I sat on one of the few available benches. I talked with the benchwarmers to my right and left but didn't make any effort to meet anyone else. Number Three approached me, chatted me up, sat next to me at the movie, and e-mailed me the next day through the meet-up website. Only a few weeks after my being dumped by Number Two, Three and I went on our first date. I couldn't believe I'd met someone new so quickly.

My relationship with Three was intense but short lived. He liked to hike, and one week we walked over twenty-seven miles. He continually expressed confusion over what he wanted and eventually broke up with me. We tried to remain friends even though I'd sworn off being friends with exes. An error in judgment, no doubt influenced by too many recent break ups: the friendship didn't last long.

Less than two months later, just as I was healing from the break-up with Three, Number Four entered my life. Initially he was lovely in every way and pursued me vigorously. I warned him of my fragile state after too many breakups and of my need to go slowly. After two weeks of dating, I went on vacation, during which we texted and spoke daily. I took many photos, mostly to show him. We had a sweet reunion when I came home. He'd been respectful of my need to proceed slowly, although he wanted to spend the night with me, with the understanding that we wouldn't be intimate. But while I'd been on vacation, he'd made a list of nine reasons we should have sex. I didn't have the heart to tell him I'd been having rocking-hot sex for months and wasn't even remotely sex starved. But his list *was* extremely seductive, and like an idiot, I let myself be lured in.

I quickly discovered that Four was great at seduction but lacked most other relationship skills. Once we began having sex, all attempts at other forms of intimacy ceased. Endlessly self-absorbed, he dropped all the interest he'd shown in becoming close and getting to know me. He could talk for over an hour about himself and never so much as ask how my day went. But I'd had too many recent breakups and couldn't face another one, which kept me in the relationship longer than was healthy.

We talked about our issues several times—too often for a new relationship. Then one pleasant Saturday night after watching one of his favorite TV shows and snuggling for hours, he told me he wanted to pull back, to continue to date, but not be so involved, i.e. less texting, calling, and seeing each other. I agreed, but added I'd be dating other people. In response, he broke up with me. Later, I realized there had been too many red flags, and our breakup had been a good thing.

It's been over a year since that first post-Simon date. I've been hit on more times that I can count, including by a twenty-three-year-old and by someone who looked like my grandfather. I've also had a handful of first dates that never went anywhere. When I told a friend I seemed to be having a strange, delayed adolescence, she stared at me and replied, "Adolescence was never like this."

I'm not the same person I was a year ago. I've been sexually self-confident since my early twenties, but now I'm confident about every aspect of my romantic life. The sheer number of men that I've dated changed my self-concept. I always marveled at women who were quickly and easily able to meet new partners, and now I've become one of those women. I had great moments with each of the men I dated this year, and collectively, these experiences were transformative. My deficits haven't changed, but my strengths have increased.

The experience is similar to my study of Tae Kwon Do. After passing the black belt test, I still clumsily walked into walls, but I was also powerful and confident. My collective dating experiences have similarly changed me.

My relationships are no longer happy accidents. I jokingly refer to my "middle- age man-candy mojo." While I'm a proponent of intentional change, not all transformation is purposeful or planned. Sometimes change is spontaneous and organic, happening because our lives are propelled forward, and we are fully engaged in that propulsion.

I remain the latest of late bloomers. But whether it is decades overdue, or perfect timing, more than anything else, I've finally matured into the woman I've always wanted to be. It feels better than I could have possibly imagined.

EPILOGUE: 2019

As I approach sixty, I've continued to date and learn new lessons about love and relationships. Although occasionally frustrated by the lack of lasting love, in retrospect, I know if I'd found it, I'd have missed out on experiences I've valued and sometimes treasured. Each relationship has brought new pleasures and lessons. My big take-aways from dating in my fifties include the following:

1. Back away quickly from confused men. If they don't know what they want when you begin to date, they probably aren't going to become more insightful during the relationship. Date men who know what they're looking for. They're less likely to use you as a stepping stone in their own evolution.

2. Stay away from moody men. If they can't put their best foot forward during the beginning stages of a relationship, they never will.

3. Avoid dating men who don't want the same things you do. You aren't going to change their needs, no matter how wonderful you are. Once you understand you're not in sync, bail quickly.

4. Don't date men who aren't over their exes. The feelings about the exes suck away too much emotional energy to allow development of a new, healthy relationship.

5. Beware of men who can't express their feelings and needs. If you choose to date them, you'll probably become responsible for all of the emotional heavy lifting in the relationship. You deserve a partner who is emotionally at your level.

6. Trust your instincts. If your gut tells you something is off, it probably is.

7. Don't forget to embrace joy. I've had two friends-with-benefits in my fifties. Each relationship lasted several years, and both brought me great happiness. If I'd decided to date only men who wanted a serious long-term relationship, I would have missed out on many blissful experiences.

8. Remember, as in *the Bridges of Madison County*, love can catch you unaware. Be open. I once met a man on the subway while vacationing in New York City. We loved each other, but the relationship didn't last. He still occasionally calls and texts. Even if the relationship doesn't endure, the good feelings may remain for the rest of your life.

9. Have faith that you're never too old or too anything (sick, busy, etc.), to have wonderful romantic experiences. I've had many great romances since my divorce, and I firmly believe there are more in my future. And when I'm not pursuing romance, you'll find me at my happy place—the movies.

REFERENCES

BOOKS

Cooper, James Fenimore. 1826. *The Last of the Mohicans*. Philadelphia, PA: H.C. Carey & I. Lea

Hays, Daniel, and Hays, David. 1995. *My Old Man and the Sea*. Chapel Hill, N.C.: Algonquin Books of Chapel Hill

Austin, Jane. 1813. *Pride and Prejudice*. London, England: T. Egerton, Military Library, Whitehall

MUSIC, TELEVISION, AND PLAYS

Dylan, Bob. (1975) *Blood on the Tracks*. New York, NY: Columbia Records

Jackson, Michael. (1982) *Thriller*. Los Angeles, CA: Westlake Recording Studios

Desperate Housewives. ABC Studios and Cherry Productions, 2004

The Sopranos. HBO, Chase Films, and Brad Grey Television, 1999

Gurney, A.R. (1989) *Love Letters*. New York, NY: Dramatists Play Service, Inc.

MOVIES

Kernochan, Sarah, Zalman King, and Patricia Louisianna Knop. *9 1/2 Weeks*. Director Adrian Lyne. 1986. USA. Galactic Films.

Arriaga, Guillermo. *21 Grams*. Director Alejandro Ganzalez Inarritu. 2003. USA. This is That Production Company.

Sweet, John. *The Affair of the Necklace*. Director Charles Shyer. 2001. USA. Alcon Entertainment.

Parker, Alan. *Angel Heart*. Director Alan Parker. 1987. USA. Tri-Star Pictures.

Ramis, Harold, Douglas Kenney, and Chris Miller. *Animal House*. Director John Landis. 1978. USA. Universal Pictures.

Marber, Patrick and Chrysanthy Balis. *Asylum*. Director David Mackenzie. 2005. United Kingdom Ireland. Paramount Classics.

Eszterhas, Joe. *Basis Instinct*. Director Paul Verhoeven. 1992. USA. TriStar Pictures.

Linkletter, Richard and Julie Delpi. *Before Sunset*. Director Richard Linkletter. 2004. USA. Warner Independent Pictures.

Mumolo, Annie and Kristen Wiig. *Bridesmaids*. Director Paul Feig. 2011. USA. Universal Pictures.

LaGravenese, Richard. *The Bridges of Madison County*. Director Clint Eastwood. 1995. USA. Amblin Entertainment.

Salt, Waldo and Robert C. Jones. *Coming Home*. Director Hal Ashby. 1978. USA. Jerome Hellman Productions Inc.

Brodin, Kevin and Frank Cappello. *Constantine*. Director Francis Lawrence. 2005. USA. Warner Brothers.

Sandler, Susan. *Crossing Delancey*. Director Joan Micklin Silver. 1988. USA. Warner Brothers.

Romero, George A. and Dario Argento. *Dawn of the Dead*. Director George A. Romero. 1978. USA. Dawn Associates.

Fonda, Peter, Dennis Hopper, and Terry Southern. *Easy Rider*. Director Dennis Hopper. USA. 1969. Raybert Productions.

De Vore, Christopher, Eric Bergren, and David Lynch. *The Elephant Man*. Director David Lynch. 1980. USA. Brooksfilms.

Grant, Susannah. Erin Brocovich. Director Steven *Soderbergh*. 2000. USA. Universal Pictures.

Kaufman, Charlie. *The Eternal Sunshine of the Spotless Mind.* Director Michel Gondry. 2004. USA. Focus Features.

Puzzo, Mario and Francis Ford Coppola. *The Godfather.* Director Francis Ford Coppola. 1972. USA. Paramount Pictures.

Resnais, Alain and Paul Eluard. *Guernica.* Director Alain Resnais and Robert Hessens. France. 1950. Les Films del la Pleiade.

Carpenter, John and Debra Hill. *Halloween.* Director John Carpenter. 1978. USA. Compass International Pictures.

Johnson, Nunnally. *How to Marry a Millionaire.* Director Jean Negulesco. 1953. USA. 20th Century Fox.

Bertolucci, Bernardo and Franco Arcalli. *Last Tango in Paris.* Director Bernardo Bertolucci. 1972. France. United Artists.

Levinson, Barry. *Liberty Heights.* Director Barry Levinson. 1999. USA. Baltimore Pictures.

Anderson, Wes and Noah Baumback. *The Life Aquatic with Steve Zissou.* Director Wes Anderson. 2004. USA. Touchstone Pictures.

Allen, Woody and Marshall Brickman. *Manhattan.* Director Woody Allen. 1979. USA. Jack Rollins and Charles H. Joffe Productions.

Taraporevala, Sooni. *Mississippi Masala.* Director Mira Nair. 1991. United Kingdom, USA. Studio Canal Souss.

Getchell, Robert, Tracy Hotchner, Frank Perry, and Frank Yablans. *Mommie Dearest.* Director Frank Perry. 1981. USA Paramount Pictures.

Nettelbeck, Sandra. *Mostly Martha.* Director Sandra Nettelbeck. 2001. Germany. Bavaria Films.

Rudolph, Alan and Randy Sue Coburn. *Mrs. Parker and the Vicious Circle.* Director Alan Rudolph. 1994. USA. Miramax.

Bass, Ronald. *My Best Friend's Wedding.* Director P.J. Hogan. 1997. USA. Zucker Brothers Productions.

Helgeland, Brian. *Mystic River.* Director Clint Eastwood. 2003. USA. Village Roadshow Picture Malpaso Productions.

Sargent, Alan. *Ordinary People.* Director Robert Redford. 1980. USA. Wildwood Enterprises, Inc.

Harwood, Ronald. *The Pianist*. Director Roman Polanski. 2002. USA. Canal+.

Lawton, J.F. *Pretty Woman*. Director Garry Marshall. 1990. USA. Touchstone Pictures.

Boaz, Yakin. *A Price Above Rubies*. Director Yakin Boaz. 1998. United Kingdom, USA. Miramax Films.

McGovern, Jimmy. *Priest*. Director Antonia Bird. 1994. United Kingdom. BBC Films.

Trumbo, Dalton, Ian McLellan Hunter, and John Dighton. *Roman Holiday*. Director William Wyler. 1953. United States. Paramount Pictures.

Tidyman, Ernest and John D. F. Black. *Shaft*. Director Gordon Parks. 1971. USA. Metro-Goldwyn-Mayer.

Tally, Ted. *The Silence of the Lambs*. Director Jonathan Demme. 1991. USA. Strong Heart/Demme Production.

Wilder, Billy and I.A.L. Diamond. *Some Like It Hot*. Director Billy Wilder. 1959. USA. Mirisch Company.

Meyers, Nancy. *Something's Gotta Give*. Director Nancy Meyers. 2003. USA. Columbia Pictures Waverly Films.

Pakula, Alan J. *Sophie's Choice*. Director Alan J. Pakula. 1982. USA. IYC Entertainment.

Kim, Ki-duk. *Spring, Summer, Fall, Winter...and Spring*. Director Ki-duk Kim. 2003. South Korea. JL Film.

Lee, Spike, Victor Coliccio, and Michael Imperiolo. *Summer of Sam*. Director Spike Lee. 1999. USA. Forty Acres and & A Mule Filmworks.

Favreau, Jon. *Swingers*. Director Jon Favreau. 1996. USA. Independent Pictures.

Khourie, Callie. *Thelma and Louise*. Director Ridley Scott. 1991. USA. Pathé Entertainment.

Malick, Terrance. *The Thin Red Line*. Director Terrance Malick. 1998. USA. Fox 2000 Pictures.

Romano, John. *The Third Miracle*. Director Agnieszka Holland. 1999. USA. American Zoetrope.

Well, Audrey. *The Truth About Cats and Dogs*. Director Michael Lehmann. USA. 1996. 20th Century Fox.

Chabrol, Claude and Alvin Sargent. *Unfaithful*. Director Adrian Lyne. 2002. USA. Fox 2000 Pictures.

Friedman, Josh and David Koepp. *War of the Worlds*. Director Steven Spielberg. 2005. Amblin Entertainment.

Ephron, Nora. *When Harry Met Sally*. Director Rob Reiner. 1989. USA. Castle Rock Entertainment.

Sullivan, Daniel G. and Fredric Lebow. *While You Were Sleeping*. Director Jon Turtleltaub.1995. USA. Buena Vista Pictures.

PLEASE REVIEW THIS BOOK

If you liked this book, please considering submitting a review to Amazon, Barnes & Noble, and GoodReads. It is difficult to get the word out about good books. Reviews help. The author and publisher will appreciate any effort you make.

Other Books by Joanna Charnas

100 Tips and Tools for Managing Chronic Illness

Living Well with Chronic Illness

Other Memoirs from
MSI Language & Culture Books

57 Steps to Paradise (Lorenz)

Blest Atheist (Mahlou)

Damascus amid the War (M. Imady)

Forget the Goal, the Journey Counts (Stites)

From Deep Within (Lewis)

Good Blood (Schaffer)

Healing from Incest (Henderson & Emerton)

It Only Hurts When I Can't Run (Parker)

Las Historias de Mi Vida (Ustman)

Of God, Rattlesnakes, and Okra (Easterling)

One Family Indivisible (Greenebaum)

One Simple Text (Shaw & Brown)

Road to Damascus (E. Imady)

Tucker and Me (Harvey)